MEAT LOVE

DISCOURSE 010

MEAT LOVE
AN IDEOLOGY OF THE FLESH

AMBER HUSAIN

INTRODUCTION

Until I was twenty-six years old, I had never looked at a piece of meat. I had seen and eaten a lot of them – countless roasted chicken legs sticky with wine; cured and ruptured sausages slickening spaghetti; spiced hunks of lamb in pools of orange oil; nuggets, rashers, burgers, schnitzels, skewers, steaks. The 'horse tartare' I ingested at a Ukrainian restaurant in Poland did not strike me in its relation to *a* horse. Before my final effort to roast a plucked and headless bird, I cannot remember seeing any item as embodied or possessed as a chicken's leg, the leg of a lamb, pigs' flesh, a cow's rump. All I remember witnessing is the juicy abstraction of 'meat'.

It was love that made me do it – both the roasting and, later, the looking that would mean my final roast. Until I was twenty-six, I had cooked and eaten for love of a meat-hungry boyfriend; I'd reassured my mother on losing too much weight by scraping hardened lamb fat from a cooled-down plate and depositing it on my tongue. Mostly, I'd eaten for my own, private love of meat itself – the easy delivery of flavour from a fatty, proteinous mass, the brilliant nostalgia held by scorch marks, crackling, and grease.

It was also love, this time of a self-described vegan, that would eventually come to estrange me from these pleasures. Their influence helped to change, if not my mind, then at least my habits. Eventually I ceased to think in terms of meat while deliberating dinner. Still then, I felt that refusing meat was little more than a salve for the naively guilty consumer. The 'cruelty-free' performances of middle-class urban individuals were, it seemed to me, an irrelevance from the perspective of any meaningful critique of our political order. For as long as our food was embedded in a system beholden to profit, driving the plunder of whatever land and life would produce the most favourable margins; for as long as that system foreclosed the equal distribution of what was produced; for as long as farmers and shoppers alike were dependent on wages to eat; for as long as all this was the case, I reasoned, animal meat would need to be bought and sold for the maintenance of human life.

Yet to slide your buttery hand between the flesh and skin of a thing that, if only for a moment, you have re-learnt to perceive as a corpse is to give an invigorating massage to your sense of political possibility. It is the kind of shock to sensory expectation that opens up more earnest consideration of alternatives to the society that produced that corpse and channelled it into your kitchen. This sensory politicisation involves, I want to suggest, a particular kind of looking.

The animals we've wanted to look at for much of post-industrial history have typically been those still living. In a 1977 essay asking 'Why Look at Animals?', the artist, art critic, poet, and leftist activist and thinker John Berger took the practice of looking at animals to be *related* to the fact of meat, yet not exactly to coincide with it. Berger's paradigm site for the spectacle of commodified animality is not the pasture, abattoir, butcher's shop, or plate – though commodities do live there – but rather, and more obviously, the zoo. Yet 'nowhere in a zoo', he observes, 'can a stranger look at an animal'. For ever since animals came to be used as industrial machines, treated as raw material for food and exhibited for human amusement, our view of them, Berger writes, has always been 'wrong'. However close you might come to an animal's face, you are looking '*at something that has been rendered absolutely marginal*'. 'All the concentration you can muster', he concludes, 'will never be enough to centralise it.' Once, that is, you have made something living into an object of one-sided encounter, you cannot expect it to present itself to you as something fascinating in its aliveness.

Animals, to Berger's mind, were either commodified as meat or commodified as spectacles. His account did not accommodate any overlapping *spectacle of meat* – the existence of which would imply an outright embrace of death-dealing violence. At the zoo, we disavow the violence behind the spectacle of profit-driven life; with meat, we tend to ignore that the thing we are consuming was ever alive. Though perhaps morally negligent, neither way of seeing could be judged as irredeemably violent. Both acts of indirect aggression seemed corrigible, Berger thought, by the power of new ways of seeing. Perhaps if, by treating animals as more than mere objects of our gaze, we began to *truly look* – to centralise their subjectivity – we might also chip away at our tendency to reduce the animal to meat.

It was forty years after the publication of Berger's essay that I found myself looking at meat and finally seeing a carcass – plucked, beheaded, and fleshy, its rear end opened to my unwaxed lemon. Proximity to the disgust of someone you desire can radicalise the stomach. But two specific conditions other than love were central to my change of heart. First, the availability to middle-class Londoners like myself of viable alternatives to nourishment by meat. Second, immersion in a culture of ideas that posited meat as murder. More broadly, an era of climate catastrophe linked with a structurally sadistic system of factory farming has shrunk the space for disavowal in the sphere of public discourse. Among those with the luxury of choice, most are convinced of the cruelties of industrialised animal farming, such that the actual embrace of violence takes only relatively marginal forms. Some on the left perceive the inadequacy of consumer choice to transforming the entire food system. The most disenchanted are wont to acknowledge their own disempowerment by eating the system's losers. Then there are others at certain extremes of the political right who would simply defend an inalienable right to exploit, extract, and consume.

Yet it is only in the five years or so since I have been able to look at meat and witness its animal nature that I've also become conscious of a practice of looking that Berger did not foresee. Namely, the eminently contemporary middle-class tendency both to look at meat *and* relish its consumption. Indeed, it is a matter of looking *all the better to eat* – an enhancement of eating pleasure both aesthetic and 'ethical' in nature. From opulently packaged deliveries of plumped and marbled flesh to cookbooks filled with offal-heavy installation art, the spectacle of the grass-fed, free-range, hand-reared, 'happy' carcass has bled its protoblack pudding into the mass cultural sphere. The image of meat as 'honest', 'traditional', 'local', 'well-fed' fare is now as much a face of supermarket chicken as rarefied urban butchery, the content of both television advertising and Instagram influencers. In *looking* at our meat – from its grain, colour, bounciness, and sheen to the ground on which it was fattened and the horizon on which it once gazed – we suppose we can redeem the cruelty that the making of meat entails. This is a cruelty perceived as wrought either by some brute 'human nature' (per the right wing) or the totalising capitalist mode of production (per the melancholic left). Stored within the spectacle of 'ethical meat' is the suggestion of a source of redemption, namely 'love'.

This love invokes an ethic of care, respect, appreciation, and mourning for the animal lives we take into our mouths and the human lives involved in getting them there. Yet the political implications of honouring this love are more complex than perhaps they first seem. While it is basic that an attitude of love will make for better farming, 'processing', and selling of meat, the necessity of doing so at all remains a matter of ideological negotiation. It should come as no surprise that those whom capitalist society has vested with the power to manage our relationship with meat are those with the greatest means of profiting from its consumption. And yet, it is in the very nature of ideology to mystify these relations – to obscure each of our positions in the system of exploitation with vaguenesses of ethic and vibe.

What I call Meat Love is both a gentrification of meat and a 'Gentrification of the Mind'. As Sarah Schulman writes in her book of that name, gentrification is a process that displaces not only people but also their perception of reality. A gentrified landscape is filled with the physical bodies of the bourgeoisie; a gentrified mind is filled with a bourgeois perspective that calls itself 'reality'. Its myth provides an illusory sense of happiness, available in return for our cooperation with injustice. The Meat-Loving gaze is supposed to be directed with compassion at the 'origins' of our food, lending these origins the benevolent aura of 'truth'. But as any bespectacled child with an impish parent will know, a lens smeared with kisses is a window primed to be filled with greasy distortions.

Industrial meat farming, while comparatively horrific in its in-built degradation of animal life, has something fundamental in common with any form of sustainable or ethical meat farming; beholden to the profit motive, both must culminate in killing for produce. At its worst, then, the ideology of Meat Love can serve more as an elevation than a mitigation of violence, an insidious innovation through which both speciesism and capitalism are embedded in common sense. The availability and popularity of lovingly 'raised' and sustainably farmed kinds of meat has no scope to undermine the economic imperatives according to which industrial meat production swells. Meanwhile, it turns out to be those we consider most 'dependent' on our care, most locked in a relationship of love, that we take as fairest game to be objectified, exploited, and killed.

In a sense, then, this book is underpinned by a materialist view of the politics of human-animal relations. It is premised on the simple observation that a love of animal life coextensive with a love of meat can liberate neither animals nor humans from the worst of capitalist violence. Yet the book's more central, and less simple, subject of inquiry is why the middle classes find ourselves so susceptible to the belief that it will. In short, it scrutinises why the romance of 'ethical' meat has gathered such cultural momentum. The ideology of Meat Love, we shall see, is an ideology of the flesh – a carnal seduction that situates animal flesh at the centre of fleshly desire.

This psychic account of human society's embroilment in animal exploitation roils the purified waters of certain leftist approaches to anti-speciesist politics. Critical theorists have tended to pit the vegan 'lifestyle choice' against the commitment to an alternative social model. In the view of Marxist animal rights activist Marco Maurizi, for instance, the problem is simply that 'veganism is not a "mode of production"': no number of virtuous eaters excising meat from their personal menus equates to a transformation of capitalist food system. Instead of fighting the *ideas* of individuals, Maurizi writes in *Beyond Nature*, a politics aimed at an equal and just relationship between animals and humans should attack 'the *material* structure of *society* that generates those ideas in the first place'. Yet can cause and effect work only in one or other direction? Ideas are certainly products, to some extent, of material structures, but the formation of material structures are equally shaped by ideas, by desires.

It is Maurizi's belief, and others' on the utopian left, that a communist social order would naturally transform inter-species relations – that a fair and just society among humans would erase the need for every form of competitive subordination. It is thus that many of those on the left who are able to commit a life's energy to 'social justice' justify an unwillingness to extend this commitment to non-human species in the capitalist present. Yet in the face of such an unwillingness, a deeply embedded disposition, can we be safe in bracketing within the cause of animal liberation with anti-capitalist struggle? So often have I witnessed resignation slide into limitless indulgence, the once-vegetarian comrade evolve into the meatiest bon viveur. It seems unlikely that meat should be naturally expunged from the communist horizon if the very communist order is to be defined by those whose passion for transformation coexists with a guiltless pleasure in feasting on animal flesh; by those who daily relish the products of animal exploitation.

As feminist thinkers have long pointed out, what is at stake is not just how much violence is wrought, but who counts as a subject of violence in the first place. There are lives, as Judith Butler writes, 'that are not quite – or indeed, are never – recognized as lives'. Such categorisations, I will propose, are matters of aesthetics, of sensual experience. On such a view, it cannot simply be the structures of society that lead to our sense of animals' edibility. For what if our everyday acts of looking and eating were also the means through which we formed ourselves as architects of these structures? This is a different kind of 'action' from the market mechanism of 'voting with one's fork' – of adopting a vegan diet in the hope that supply will simply follow demand. Rather, it is a matter of orienting ourselves as active political beings towards the very overhaul of market society.

This book is an account of how, in coaxing meat through our digestive tracts again and again, the ideology of Meat Love teaches us to embody an embrace of exploitation in a spirit of virtuous indulgence – an embrace that inevitably ramifies in concrete political structures. In what follows I attempt to approach this ideology, absorbing its aesthetic features, in the two-way manner with which I perceive my own lurch towards non-carnivorousness. Just as one's specific way of 'looking' at meat is related to both culture and class, the ideology of Meat Love must be understood as a matter of both in interaction; a matter of perpetual interplay between representation and 'structure', a case of both how we experience meat and how we are allowed to.

If then, as I will argue, the aesthetics of Meat Love are imbued with certain ideals – of tragedy, harmony, and beauty in the loving rendering of flesh – such representational ideals on the one hand *inform* how we come to think of ourselves as a class of meat-eating humans and on the other *depend* on the material realities of class for their representational power. As Louis Althusser suggested in his theory of ideology, the ideas that dominate the minds of specific social groups are images of our relationship to the class society, fantastical and ritual in nature, yet are always imagined within limits that are set by productive forces. We are witness to a powerful aesthetic campaign of carnivorous interests, embellishing the image of meat with values of intelligence, kindness, and stewardship, albeit a stewardship that offers us increasingly catastrophic evidence of its returns. We are more or less likely to respond to this campaign according to various complexities – our politics perhaps, but constrained by the facts of material existence – the things that must be done to make money, build networks of kinship and eat to survive.

Yet despite these complexities, and despite the fact that Meat Love has come to constitute a profound new way of seeing – so does a belligerent resistance to Meat Love surface through the cracks of our visual culture. If the ideal form of this resistance comes with the attempt to transform the social order, such efforts are always entangled with aesthetics – perceptions, attitudes, ways of being. Embodied in our acts of creativity, not least concerning what we eat, these are central to our capacity for rejecting capitalism's systematic devaluation of life – a hierarchical devaluation as brutal at any given historical moment as the profit motive requires. To reject the ideology of Meat Love would be to foster a world in which the products of violence and exploitation could no longer be objects of need or desire; a world in which no-one, neither animal, immigrant, worker, woman, or peasant, was considered a thing to be owned, controlled, killed, or left to die.

Millions visit the zoo, writes Berger, 'out of a curiosity which [is] both so large, so vague and so personal that it is hard to express it in a single question'. The same could be said of our modern fascination with the spectacle of meat. What follows is an attempt to distil the chaos of questions into one. Love has always been capable of meaning many things, among them a propensity to kill. If love is somehow newly compatible with meat, what kind of lovers have we become?

TRAGEDY

If there is drama in John Berger's story about the killing of a pig, there is very little suspense. At the heart of Berger's book *Pig Earth* (1979), the fictional fruit of his time living among a peasant community in France, Pépé, the protagonist's grandfather, announces to his family that 'tomorrow we are going to kill the pig'. In the sequence that follows, every character, pig included, is shown to understand their role.

The pig, until then, has complied with being fed 'like one of the family', albeit one who is destined for the chop. But now, at a quasi-majestic hundred and forty-two kilos, his feeding days are up. Seeing grandma in the kitchen doorway without her bucket of food, he immediately perceives his fate. For the very first time, he hesitates, then lunges and kicks, 'like a man', like 'a man fighting off robbers'.

They say it takes a village to raise a child and the same can be true of killing. Neighbours assemble to help with hauling the noose around the pig's neck, to resist the force of his gigantic hams and midwife his surrender with their fists. 'During the next twelve months', the child-narrator explains, 'he was going to give body to our soup, flavour our potatoes, stuff our cabbages, fill our sausages. His hams and rolled breast, salted and dried, were going to lie on the rack, suspended from the ceiling above Pépé and Mémé's bed.' The pig is both loved and lamented by those who would otherwise starve. The fatal cut is made and his screams become deep breaths.

One of the most striking images in the film adaptation of *Pig Earth* is that of the pig's head, its severance the decisive moment of becoming meat. As stills of the annual slaughter mount onscreen, we witness the smiling corpse as he is hauled onto a sledge. One moment his head is attached to a recently animate being, the next it is a thing – a manufactured theatrical prop.

Such props are not unfamiliar in visual culture of meat. In Western theatre, perhaps the most ubiquitous head to be seen is that of Pentheus in Euripides' tragic drama *The Bakkhai*. In that play, first produced in 405 BCE, the King of Thebes and his mother are punished for refusing to acknowledge Dionysus, god of nature and its pleasures, horns on his head and snakes in his hair. Dionysus lures the women of Thebes (including King Pentheus's mother Agave) into the mountains where he gets them high. Having done so he invites a fusty, disapproving Pentheus up there with him to confront the women face to face. It is there, through his female followers, that Dionysus will harvest revenge. In true tragic style, it is Agave herself who will glean her son's head from his body.

For the revelling, outward-bound bakkhai, ancient, elemental customs sprouting from nature are as valid as civilising law. Leaving their children at home, they are as happy cradling and suckling wolf cubs and fawns as they are pulling calves to pieces, scattering chunks of flesh as they stumble among the herds. Meat and love are the intertwined pillars of a life dictated by a god. It is only 'natural', then, in the world of the play, that Pentheus should be loved as meat.

When Agave finally tears the head of her beloved son from his neck, she is apparently 'out of her mind'. She

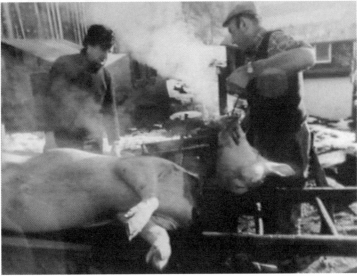

Stills from *Pig Earth*, directed by Mike Dibb, 1979

does not hear him identify himself as she plants her foot on his chest and rips the meat from his bones. Picking up his head and impaling it on a stick as though it were a mountain lion's, she crows with pride at her hunting success and descends to display it for her son. Finally, in one of ancient Greek theatre's least watchable comings-to, she sees what she has done and howls, herself most painfully undone. Berger's peasant child howls too when he wakes the day after the killing to re-witness the head he was handed and dutifully put on ice. He howls as he is properly acquainted with the frozen face of the 'family' he helped to dispatch.

Many are the tragic tales in which some form of necessity brings meat together with love. For the peasants who populate *Pig Earth*, it is a necessity of life that the animal be both loved and slaughtered. In *The Bakkhai* it is vengeful nature's demand that the same be true of Pentheus. Yet the 'drama', such as it is, is not to be found in the inevitable act of killing. Rather it rises and falls as the necessity of killing is contested by the victims of power. The pig, before he is made invisible beneath a heap of men, discovers strength he has never known before; his legs begin to lunge with 'desperate speed and force' and his yells

Agave (Sarah Walker) with the severed head of her murdered son Pentheus in *The Bakkhai*, English National Opera, London, 1992

begin to escalate in volume. Pentheus too begs for mercy as his murderous mother, a proxy for the god, foams over him from her mouth. In every act of struggle we witness an attack and a defence of what can rightly be butchered. If the starkest act of domination is to make another into meat, *The Bakkhai* puts the meat-worthy subject continually up for grabs. To Dionysus, it is Pentheus who has meatiest potential; to Pentheus, the animal is Agave; to Agave there is no one lowlier than herself but livestock – heifers, sheep, and calves. Pentheus is out to defend the right of law; Agave sets out to contest it. Pentheus contests the right of Dionysus; the god defends it most horribly. Once the pig in *Pig Earth* has been scraped of all hair with the sides of tablespoons, he reminds the villagers not of a pig, nor any man among them, but of a 'man of leisure', he who typically profits from the land – fatter, pink, and untanned, a looming bigger Other.

As with pigs and peasants, there is always a loser in the tragic exercise of power. The drama crests at that moment of realisation on the part of the 'weak' that things are about to go south. It is tragedy's most awful treat to its blood-lustful audience that attempts at love are set on a relentless course to culminate in meat. If meat and love are by any indomitable force brought into contact, that force is typically violent.

As Berger himself puts it in the afterword to *Pig Earth*, 'However much a bad harvest is considered an act of God, however much the master/landowner is considered a natural master … the basic fact is clear: they who can feed themselves are instead being forced to feed others.' By 'peasants', he refers to those whose 'surplus' production of food is a condition of their survival. Like the produce of pre-enclosure peasants, which went first to a lord and the remainder to the peasants themselves (on which they hoped to subsist), that which is produced by the modern peasant is gobbled by the market economy. Peasant life, Berger writes, is characterised by rituals and routines that attempt 'to wrest some meaning … from a cycle of remorseless change' – a cycle which, by the time of his writing in the 1970s, consists of feeding an unwieldy economic system.

Indeed, with the intensification of capitalist production comes the intensification of both human and animal exploitation. The early needs of industry led to the mass

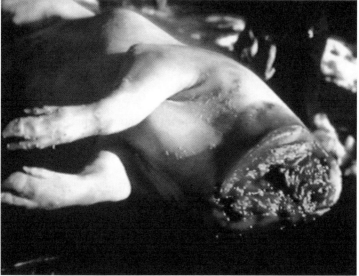

Stills from *Pig Earth*, directed by Mike Dibb, 1979

displacement of peasants; later the needs of industrial agriculture led to the mass expropriation of their land, cheap labour, and food. The present agricultural order, equally driven by growth, must find ever more technologised ways to destroy the planet, human wellbeing, and animal life. Global meat production has more than tripled since the time of Berger's writing, and is predicted to double again in the next thirty years. Modern capitalism's separation of life from nonhuman nature, recruiting animal and land into the process of profit-driven manufacture, has culminated in a fossil-fuel-dependent, land-hungry, chemically fertilised frenzy of animal cruelty, organised by a corporate class with relatively little motive to care.

However they are eventually killed, the farmed female pigs of today may swell at human hands to over two hundred kilograms only to live their fattened lives in the modest spaces those hands apportion. The least fortunate gestate their young in cages or 'crates' and wait to be inseminated again, never long after their piglets have been taken away. When they are sent to be killed, pigs of either gender are often stuffed into holding crates, squealing in dissent as they go. Once they have been stunned and hung up from their legs, they are finally stabbed in the neck, after which point they continue to struggle for further tens of seconds.

In the era of *Pig Earth* in the Europe Berger describes, the urban industrial workforce and middle-class diners alike were united in a certain insulation from the facts of rural life. If industrialisation had introduced to the 'citizen' security, permanence, protection – in the form of heating, transport, laws, and other such defences against nature's vicissitudes – so had it also shielded their hearts and minds from the realities of animal farming. The cosseting of this citizen had now become so 'total' as to suffocate imagination of the land. 'Alone in a serviced limbo', to use Berger's terms, the urban consumer, having never been expected to love the pigs he would eat, could no longer even be expected to acknowledge their having lived at all.

Berger warns any reader liable to be rapt in bucolic nostalgia against romanticisation of the lost peasant class. He is loath to brandish the peasant as an idol to be preserved, since to do so would preserve his exploitation. Nevertheless, he fears what it might mean for humankind to obliterate manual farming. Where previously cities were dependent on the countryside for food, soon, Berger predicted, the countryside would be dependent on the cities for the means of survival. This would mark an end for the peasant's unique understanding of the real 'value' of nature, the cost to the earth of capitalism's use of land and life. It was Berger's prediction in the late 1970s that another twenty years would unfold in a similar direction to that which he had seen in the 1950s and '60s.

Yet in fact, twenty odd years from then, if an urban citizen of the industrialised West thirsted to return to the land, a media movement was rushing to meet them in their home. In the UK, for instance, the metropolitan consumer needed look no further than Channel 4. It was there, in 1999, that the charming urban cherub named Hugh Fearnley-Whittingstall took to the screen to help popularise, or perhaps reconstruct, a dwindling smallholder consciousness. In the series *Escape to River Cottage*, we follow Hugh as he moves from London to Dorset to model the labours of small-scale farming, throwing himself into a life of building and growing, bartering and market-stall hawking, and raising and 'finishing' livestock. If the witlessly insulated urban dolt lived a life surrounded by supermarket meat – slabs of glistening pastel pink so far from the blood of butchery – Hugh was here to show us where that alienated flesh expressly *hadn't* come from. Hugh was here to save our souls from financing the bloodbath of factory farming, guiding us instead to lovely River Cottage, a stable of animal love.

How does one raise the consciousness of automated, meat-pumped yuppies to register the love of the farmer, at least the 'good' one, for his pig? Hugh, an Eton- and Oxford-educated man, elected, as I have, to reference certain classical aesthetics. Having witnessed his purchase of two nice hogs at the start of *Escape to River Cottage*, six months and six episodes later, a finely wrought tragedy concludes.

Tragic doom is signalled from the first in Hugh's casual invocation of fate. Specifically, he is anxious re: the 'logistics of the fate of his pigs'. It is common in tragic drama for destiny to roll its tyres over rational deliberation. 'What should I do?' a character asks, though no amount of reasoned debate, in this genre, can lead to a happy resolution. New European legislation ordains that pigs raised for sale can no longer be killed at home, and must therefore go to an abattoir. For Hugh, the matter for internal discussion is whether to go with them.

He seems to think he has been spared the ordeal of choice when it comes to the biggest question. The question of whether or not they should be killed at all is never a subject for discussion. He needs their meat, he claims, for his winter store, and to pay back some neighbourly debts. Since pork is his prime currency, the slaughterhouse it must be. Conjuring a quintessentially peasant-shaped situation of both economic and nutritional need, Hugh opts to immerse himself fully in all the drama of mortality. 'I was there at the beginning', he concludes in a one-man choral lament, 'and I feel I ought to be there at the end.'

In Greek drama, such heroics typically lay the foundation for an imminent 'reversal': some plot-driven horror that will prove our otherwise reasonable protagonist wrong. Not that there is ever anything a hero can do to avoid the tragic conclusion. Like Clytemnestra in Aeschylus's *Agamemnon*, Hugh sets out on a slaughterous course that is reduced, in narrative terms, to the fulfilment of rituals choreographed by gods. When Hugh builds a tunnel-visioned, slip-proof bridge that will lead the pigs into the back of a truck, it is as though to re-enact Clytemnestra's rolling out of the original red carpet. It was only through the lure of said carpet that she could guide her husband, the titular King Agamemnon, to his death, which she deals him in retribution for his sacrifice of their daughter. While the King had acted under duress (divinely punished for an ancestor's child-eating crimes), he is nevertheless blamed for having laid his progeny out 'like a goat-kid over the altar'. Disputing this treatment of human life, of kin no less, like a beast appropriate for murder, Clytemnestra resolves to lay her husband out for sacrifice in the bath. Instead of Hugh's straw, she strews the way with beautiful fabrics and bids her love step inside a house that is thoroughly cursed. Clytemnestra needs nothing but flattery to lubricate the will of the gods. Hugh, having underfed his swine in advance of the special occasion, must tempt them with a bucket of pignuts.

When we next see Hugh's pigs, or more accurately their hams, being salted in the River Cottage bath, the proxy-peasant remarks on the resemblance of the scene to a 'bizarre religious ceremony'. And yet, for all its air of sacrificial pomp, the stage is utterly bloodless. As in Greek tradition, the killing itself does not take place within view – Hugh's pig trailer simply disappears into a gleaming tunnel of thickets – yet nor is there a monologue recounting the act, a typical tragic dénouement. Rather than put too literal an image to 'where the meat comes from', the emphasis swivels instead to how it is tenderly carved into bits.

Myriad opportunities here arise to congratulate the loving butcher. In the tragic form it is often bragging, or *hubris*, 'excessive boldness', that symptomatises the poverty of human self-knowledge, always with devastating outcomes. Pentheus shows hubris in wielding his kingly power unaware that he is dealing with a god. Agave is hubristic in the carefree ripping spree that leads to a dismembered son. Agamemnon is hubristic in thinking he can return to a wife whose daughter he has killed. She too is hubristic in killing him, and will later be killed by their son. For Hugh, only a 'tinge of sadness' goes hand in hand with what he describes as 'a fair measure of pride'. Yet pride is here stripped of any possible connotation of excess. Indeed, we bask in it warmly. Hugh would like to think, he muses, that he has

Stills from *Escape to River Cottage*, directed by Billy Paulett, 1999

raised 'two of the happiest pigs who ever lived in Dorset'. What fun would it be to disagree?

Despite, then, Hugh's tributes to tragic ideas of humanity and fate, the programme gives little sense of there being any kind of victim. Once he has strapped on the yoke of that fateful tragic killing, the 'loser' is neither the exploited peasant farmer who loved his pigs nor the pigs who loved to be alive. As the butcher helps our cheerful smallholder, only electively in debt, to make sure he uses every last scrap of meat, he remarks of the gaping bodies that now hang from the River Cottage ceiling that they've obviously been very well fed. In what follows each gleaming cut is cleaved into abstraction and thrust before the camera, almost as though it were a birth. As we swallow the visual goodness of this ethically farmed feast, Hugh himself stops to gaze upon the culinary potential of 'the noblest and tastiest animal ever reared for food'.

'Cooking is a daily drama', writes Hugh himself in the introduction to his biblically authoritative 2004 tome on *River Cottage Meat*, 'still staged in almost every home.' Meat eating at its worst (i.e., the eating of what is affordable, readily available, farmed with state subsidies, and culturally sanctioned) is, for Hugh, 'an ignominious expression of greed, indifference, and heartlessness'. By contrast, the smallholder's face-to-face confrontation of death is of no such moral or political consequence. No hubris taints this happier brand of tragic philosophical drama, on the grounds that, in the absence of sadist brutality in the method itself, there is nothing inherently wrong with killing if the victim isn't human.

Indeed, unlike in tragedy proper, the world of ethical meat defies any sense of blurriness in human/animal boundaries. Instead, it displays the perspective of an eternal human victor, appointed, of course, by the human himself. Hugh presents this perspective as something of a logical given. 'For hundreds of thousands of years we have hunted animals', he writes, 'and for tens of thousands we have farmed them, so that we can eat their meat ... There is continuity in our meat eating and it is, in some deep-rooted, even hard-wired, way, natural. And yet, he notes, for all our natural continuity with animals' carnivorous habits, our genteel manner of killing is markedly different from theirs. Counting no Agave among humankind, Hugh points out that we humans restrain ourselves from chasing down animals and ripping them with claws. Instead, we 'prod and poke them into a reasonably orderly queue' before stunning them into submission and dispatching them. Everyone, farmer and pig, is seemingly here at peace with his timeless, god-given role. Hugh the humane is precisely animal enough to justify killing other beings, yet humanly distinct enough to justify a claim to beneficence in doing so.

✗

Michael Pollan, *The Omnivore's Dilemma: The Secrets Behind What You Eat* (Young Readers Edition), 2015

Just when *The River Cottage Meat Book* was throwing its weight around bourgeois homes, a veritable meat 'revolution' was gestating in the USA. From scientific journalist Michael Pollan, we saw at least a gesture towards the problematisation of the 'natural' superiority of man. Much like Fearnley-Whittingstall, America's archetypical tragic hero was deeply concerned by the industrial production of burgers. But for Pollan, the readymade model of human supremacy was less an explanation for the violence involved in meat than something in itself to be explained. Pollan beckoned audiences deeper into shallow renditions of tragic complexity. In his bestselling book *The Omnivore's Dilemma* (2006), he describes a richly incongruous photograph of meat that gives him pause for meditation:

A hunter in an orange sweater is kneeling on the ground behind a pig the side of whose head has erupted in blood that is spreading like a river delta toward the bottom of the frame. The hunter's rifle is angled just so across his chest; clearly he is observing some hoary convention of the hunter's trophy portrait. One proprietary hand rests on the dead animal's broad flank. The man is looking into the camera with an expression of unbounded pride, wearing a shit-eating grin that might have been winning, if perhaps incomprehensible, had the bloody carcass sprawled beneath him been cropped out of the frame.

The *dramatis personae* described in this tragicomic display are Pollan himself and a pig he has recently shot. 'If I didn't know better', Pollan goes on, 'I would have said that the man in the picture was drunk.' Burying his avowed self-knowledge yet deeper in the third person, he muses that perhaps he was: he may have been 'captured in the throes of some sort of Dionysian intoxication'.

We shall leave aside the fact that Pollan, describing this 'subsistence hunt' for 'just enough to make a nice dinner', has already informed us that his two fellow hunters

Still from *Pig Earth*, directed by Mike Dibb, 1979

and he, over a picnic lunch involving seven types of meat, have taken in 'naturally, a bottle each of red and white wine'. The point he is trying to make in invoking intoxication is that it is possible to occupy simultaneously more than one variety of consciousness. Pollan is thrilled to have shot the pig, but nonetheless sobered by the thought of his own murderous potential. Gilding this thought with reference to Dionysus, he blames this ambivalence on nature.

The device is one that Pollan has run with for over a decade. In his 2016 Netflix series *Cooked*, in which the image of dilemma-soaked hunting is given the full cinematic treatment, a flattened pig's carcass – a subject-cum-object which Pollan feels has 'not yet become meat' is splayed before him on a barbecue. What Fearnley-Whittingstall takes for granted as the human/animal boundary, Pollan chews on extensively before coming to the same old conclusion. Whether he is standing hand on flank before a fresh, still bloodied corpse or gazing down on a butterflied body, at once sacral and humiliated, spread cruciform over charcoal, Pollan is unable to take for granted the difference between animal and man. The pig he shoots, he is unsettled to see as its body is hauled onto a tree-rigged scale,

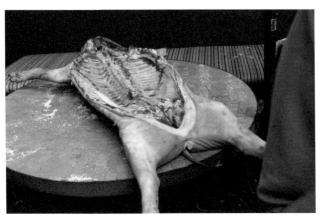

Still from *Cooked*, directed by Alex Gibney, 2016

weighs precisely the same as he does (without his gun). He is disgusted by the smell of the viscera, of the contents of the pig's intestines – precisely that which reminds him that 'we are beasts too – animals that urinate, defecate, copulate, bleed, die, stink, and decompose'.

[Yet for Pollan, there emerges a firm conviction that in 'looking', man can be redeemed. To feel he has satisfactorily respected an animal in its similarity to himself, Pollan finds it helpful to stare at what he kills, expressing gratitude for its 'gift' as though such a thing were willingly given.] This is how things are', says Clytemnestra, refusing to account for the morality of her husband's murder. While 'what is', for Pollan, is not sufficient as an answer to animal killing, it nonetheless points us in the direction from which we came – 'to that place and time … where humans *looked* at the animals they killed, regarding them with reverence.'

There is looking, and then there is cooking; the ultimate ritual through which man supposedly establishes his dominance. If Pollan is unconvinced that the pig on his barbeque is not yet a piece of meat, it takes nothing more than lighting it up to convince him of its meaty inanimacy. 'Cooking with fire', he explains with much solemnity,

> is this great reaffirmation of our very special place in the cosmos. As humans we are halfway between gods and the animals. The animals can't cook, and the gods love sacrifice. The man who wields the fire is sending that sacrifice up to the gods in the form of smoke, and declaring his elevation above the animals, who don't know how to cook, who don't know how to please the gods.

As barbeques and blowtorches light up the screen, Pollan rhapsodises on the 'complexity' afforded by the chemical reaction involved in cooking meat. In a tragic aesthetics masterfully cleansed of any of tragedy's violence, complexity of flavour melds with an apparent sophistication of thought. We too will hopefully be left with a satisfying aftertaste – the edifying sense of having made contact with a man who understands something profound: the circle of life and death, and the charcoal perimeter that demarcates the 'beast'.

It is for similarly flattering insights that Fearnley-Whittingstall chooses to illustrate his meat book's introduction with a sequence of photographs of his North Devon beef cattle being slaughtered. It is a mark of his superior sensibility, the author feels, that unlike those whose cheap burgers have been 'recovered from slaughter-house slurry', he is willing to load up his cows, watch them queue, watch them die, and then watch them be skinned and sawn in half for superior steaks. In the River Cottage pig 'processing' drama, the quartered heads of each hog replace the totemic disembodied head that stores the tragedian's supply of horror. Garlanded with herbs like living bakkhai, they simmer in a pot with spices for 'at least five hours' to be made into a thinking-man's pâté.

In recent years, the term 'meat paradox' has emerged for what psychologists describe as the 'emotional complexity' of meat – the seeming contradiction in human empathy for animals combined with a desire to eat their flesh. Rob Percival, head of food policy for the Soil Association, wrote an entire book in a bid to take this conundrum as seriously as possible. In *The Meat Paradox: Eating, Empathy and the Future of Meat* (2022), the terms in which Percival describes this human psychological curiosity are strikingly similar to those in which philosophers describe the 'paradox of tragedy' – namely, how is it that the audience member takes pleasure in theatrical spectacles of abject pain? This mystification, going back at least to Aristotle's *Poetics*, is part of what elevates tragedy in the hearts of so many aesthetes. The ultra-posh commentariat on ethical meat are similarly prone to luxuriating in the 'paradox' of grass-fed steak. When Percival witnesses the killing of a cow,

> it is as though a stone has been thrown into a pool, and the splash has ebbed, but the surface is moving still. I

Spreads from Hugh Fearnley-Whittingstall, *The River Cottage Meat Book*, 2004

> could feel those ripples, lapping against the nape of
> my neck, as though the cow's soul-stuff, thrown from
> her body in the decisive moment, was swelling upon my
> skin, searching for a shore upon which to land.

These verbal acrobatics do not aim, the author assures us, to lead us to a rational conclusion. He has written a book on meat in the pursuit of 'immersion, a visceral encounter'.

It is interesting, then, that by the end of the book, the goal has harmonised neatly with Fearnley-Whittingstall's and Pollan's, and any number of other self-appointed Meat Love educators. For having trawled various sites of animal slaughter, Percival, an omnivore now steeped in ideas of redemptive 'self-understanding', declares that we have all along been stalking a Paleolithic ideal, visible to those who would *only look*. Invoking the image of the Lion Man, a humanoid statuette with leonine head carved from a mammoth's tusk, Percival concludes that this hybrid figure is the very embodiment of the meat paradox, containing 'our' contradictions and locating them in nature. 'We long', he writes, 'for meat to be denuded of complexity, free from emotional conflict and ethical contradiction.' This, he sagely informs us, simply cannot be. Was this the intimate understanding of nature Berger worried would die along with the peasant, competed out of existence by the muscular arms of Big Agra?

What all of these animal-/meat-lovers fail to confront as they indulge in tragic aesthetics is that the so-called 'paradox of tragedy' imputes no particular complexity to the act of killing itself. Philosophers of tragedy tend to agree that the audience's implication in the horrors they see unfold are riddled with contingencies of sympathy, identification, political orientation, and emotional need. The horrors themselves, however, are invariably simple. The hierarchies of might that make it 'hubris' for an ancient Greek man to dishonour a god, a woman to dishonour a man, and a slave to dishonour a Greek woman are not particularly difficult to grasp. Nor is the idea that a social order built on the exercise of power will result in endless chains of needless bloodshed.

✕

Why, then, should those who saunter at the top of contemporary human hierarchies of power perceive a rarefied complexity in their own relationship to animal life? The tendency is surely a testament to the dwindling, since Berger's animal texts, of anything resembling class consciousness. Berger's account of the peasant is given not as a crude ventriloquism but as an analysis of the peasant's implication in the economic system. It is, after all, through this system that the production and consumption of food, meat included, must always pass. 'A peasant becomes fond of his pig and is glad to salt away its pork', writes Berger in 'Why Look at Animals?'. 'What is so difficult for the urban stranger to understand is that the two statements in that sentence are connected by an *and* and not by a *but*.' While Fearnley-Whittingstall is certainly at once endeared to his pigs and salt-happy, his particular breed of gladness, tragically conflicted, is in fact quite distinct from that which Berger describes.

This may have something to do with the fact that Hugh Fearnley-Whittingstall, unlike an actual peasant, was born of the landed gentry – the British social class whose 'living off the land' is historically a matter not of work, but of rent extraction. When he impishly speaks of 'debts' repayable only in pork, he is just as aware as his audience that this claim to material necessity is merely televisual performance. Yet what he fails to recognise is the chasm between the readiness of the peasant, the most exploitable class of human, to kill *a pig* and the universal entitlement of Man to kill Pig. One has to do with need, and how its violent imposition necessitates violence further down the hierarchy; the other has to do with an establishment of social power and its shrouding in 'laws of nature'.

As it is Berger's mission to convey, the conservatism of peasants has nothing in common with that of a privileged ruling class, nor indeed that of a 'sycophantic petty-bourgeoisie'. While bourgeois conservatism, he writes, is 'a way of siding with the powerful in exchange for a little delegated power over other classes', the conservatism of the upper classes represents an attempt, 'however vain, to make their privileges absolute'. Peasant conservatism, meanwhile, has no privilege to defend, merely the meaningfulness of a lifestyle so long imposed as to appear without alternative.

The same could of course be said of the peasant's relationship with meat. While the contemporary upper- and middle-class eater may have a pseudo-peasant's attunement to the nature and vicissitudes of rural animal farming, their positions in the capitalist system could not be more different. Ironically, in fact, it is their relative power in relation to the peasant that sustains both their capacity to play at peasantry and their financial reward for doing so. Thus, however concerned the Meat Lover may seem, or indeed feel, with the ethics of small-scale farming, he remains ironically invested in the very same mode of production whose growth necessitates animal cruelty. It is capital's need to expand that leads to the dispossession of peasant land and the exploitation of peasant, smallholder, and other agricultural labour. This includes the hyper-exploitation of factory-farmed animals, whose welfare will always be at odds with the need to expand profit margins.

As consumers, the middle classes may be more aware than ever of where our meat originates, and thus more conscious than ever of the killing it involves. Yet rather than resisting this basic devaluation of life – a devaluation that defines our classed economic order – we have attempted, by staring this fact in the face, to come to 'complicated' terms with its violence. While, for some, the encounter with meat is a particular case of survival, for others it has meant concocting a universal ethics of killing-as-love.

✗

Hugh Fearnley-Whittingstall is not the only man to have convinced himself he is a peasant, even if relatively few others have dressed up as one for a televised medieval fayre. Rob Percival, meanwhile, deduces his omnivorous ethics from the wisdom of the Tukano people, a group of Indigenous South Americans in the northwest Amazon. Surrounding himself with Tukano children as they gather to give thanks for their platters of monkey flesh, Percival extrapolates from this ritual of subsistence the nebulous tragic concept of *catharsis*. Though there is no consensus on the term's translation from Greek, one convincing interpretation is the momentary cleansing of a viewer's violent impulse when confronted with the ugliness of that impulse onstage. For Percival, however, *catharsis* or 'purification' is simply a release when the 'emotional tensions' of meat become overwhelming. 'I have returned repeatedly to the Tukano', our organic white-British soil bro explains, 'because I find their navigation of the meat paradox to be singularly sophisticated'. We must assume it is this identification, along with his concern for the protein requirements of pregnant women, that grounds Percival's elevation of his own meat-eating to a mark of superior self-knowledge.

An equally fertile fantasy is Pollan's self-alignment with Aboriginal hunter-gatherers. It is through them that, in *Cooked*, he ratifies his classic theory of hunterly virtue. The equivalence surely makes sense to the author of *The Omnivore's Dilemma*, the book in which Pollan lauds hunting as a conduit to timeless and otherwise inaccessible truths. Having determined to conquer a pig ('My Pig', as he will come to call it), the author narrates the drama, on achieving his goal, of understanding the irony-defying universal truths in José Ortega y Gasset's *Meditations on Hunting*. For one, that animality is a 'mystery' – 'one of the central mysteries of human life'. For another, that ambivalence and ambiguity have probably always been 'the hunter's lot'. Hence he proceeds from his pig-shooting experience, commingling delight and disgust, to happily conclude that this dissonance is what should 'commend' the questionable practice. His rarefied pleasure in eating its meat is marred only by his pity for the 'moral clarity of the tofu eater'. 'Dreams of innocence are just that', he writes. 'They usually depend on a denial of reality that can be its own form of hubris.'

We are used to hearing human nature described in terms of ruthless competition. If indeed, this is how we understand it, then the slaughter of one's own pigs, or indeed the eating of organic, grass-fed, free-range, or otherwise 'happy' meat, can be construed as the most commendable accommodation to that brutal fact. Any outright rejection of meat-eating can thus be framed as hopelessly naive. When Berger asks 'Why Look at Animals?', he asks us call into question our very understanding of nature. Does an animal held in the zoo really make for a plausible totem of the 'natural' world? Berger helps us to understand the futility of attempting to truly 'see' any creature, which, having been made a commodity, is 'natural' only in the most qualified of senses. What meat-thinkers such as Pollan and Fearnley-Whittingstall hope to achieve in advocating 'looking' at our meat is to defend the commodification of animal bodies as the essence of nature itself.

What is needed, goes the logic of Meat Love, to blot out the scourge of factory-farmed meat, is not a basic right to food or redistribution of wealth and agricultural subsidies but rather 'education' of the masses to understand the nature of the land – and to understand the complex means by which human 'need' must be balanced with love for nature's bounty. What is inevitably implied by 'need' is the unqualified right of those who live amid relative plenty to exploit, extract from, and ultimately consume any animal at will. However ancient the natural laws invoked by proponents of 'ethical meat', no system of social organisation has ever universalised need in these terms other than modern capitalism.

As Marx himself states at the opening of *Capital*, the commodity form translates myriad conceptions of human 'need' and 'want' into a standard expression of value. The nature of such wants, he observes, makes no difference to whether a commodity is desirable on the market, 'whether for instance they spring from the stomach or from fancy'. For those with a vested interest in the sale of meat and milk, it thus makes perfect sense to exploit the meaning of bodily need that refers specifically to food as the source of essential nutrition. Health, self-respect, even survival are offered to the guilty conscience as lenses through which to experience the purchase of what is merely desired. Images of Meat Love, whether they be targeted at the hungry or, more typically, at those who enjoy nutritive abundance, can thus become sites where ideas of need, fate, necessity, and other tragic-sounding concepts can flourish.

Of course, human needs, much like relations of animal-human domination are always socially, geographically, and historically proposed and contested. Over millennia, different species have been domesticated and hunted. Humans have formulated different ways of defining uses and needs, and different ways of articulating them to relations between humans and animals. Our current 'free' labour market is no more natural or eternal than the Bacchanalian practice of drunkenly clawing at heifers. If, then, the peasant both loves his pig and celebrates his death, what if this were less the mark of some beautifully complex, elemental 'paradox of meat' than a simple, regrettable feature of economic brutality?

This possibility is not lost on our typical pseudo-tragedian, who routinely manifests a tacit understanding of his own unforced violence – or more precisely, hints at the frisson of transgressive power that makes this violence so compulsive and seductive. It is there in the eyebrow-lifting smirk with which Hugh of *Escape to River Cottage* describes getting his hands into a bucket of blood set aside for black pudding. Tragic as the killing may be, little time is lost in marking the passage of his pigs into bodies. It is there when Pollan describes his failure to look solemn with his freshly shot pig, his effective inability to 'untie the knot' of his smile. It is little wonder that the bourgeois ethical meat-lover remains so attached to the carnivorous habits of those without his own luxury of choice. We need not wonder why the 'conscious carnivore' so rarely expresses an interest in the sovereignty of peasant farmers over the land they work and its products, in colonial displacement or gentrification, in the assurance of affordable vegetables or grains for those who live in urban food deserts. To make these his concern would deprive him of a central justification for his own more spurious pleasure.

Tragedies of Meat Love are consummate in concealing humans' psychic enchantment with the exercise of force. Sentiment, poetry, and drama, obscuring the pedestrian truth, culminate most often in moments of theatrical *recognition*. Yet whereas in the Greek tradition recognition, or *anagnorisis*, describes the transformation of deluded hope into a realisation of doom, the journey of the ethical carnivore in contemporary culture generally leads to an epiphany that meat-eating is, by whatever contortion, the *honourable* thing to do. If Percival's eureka moment takes place in encounter with the usefully ambiguous Lion Man, Pollan's occurs as he gazes on a photo of his pig once strung, newly dead, from a tree:

> I realized that here in this single picture you could actually observe the food chain in its totality ... For there was the oak tree standing in the sun, light which it had transformed into the acorns that littered the ground and fed the pig that the man in the picture was turning into food. The man had done nothing to create this food chain, only stepped into a role prepared long ago for the Predator.

In a particularly remarkable scene in *Cooked*, an animal rescuer turned 'ethical livestock farmer' describes the moment of enlightenment that changed the course of her life. Livestock farming, our convert proposes, is an especially nice way 'to live in the present, savour the past and be excited about the future'. We are treated to some ukulele and other muzakal relief as the butcher onto whom this farmer shifts her pigs carves them up into exciting, life-affirming pieces. What she says presents a striking inversion of the description of the tragic sensibility given by philosopher Simon Critchley. 'Tragic consciousness', Critchley writes, 'is staged in relation to demands that exceed autonomy, that flow from the past, disrupt the present and disable the future.'

There is a sense in which every theatrical tragedy, whether faithful to tradition or not, contains within its trajectory a story of love and meat. For if tragedies, as an almost tedious number of playwrights want to suggest, are stories of 'becoming human', such a feat has never been possible without the animal Other. 'Politics supposes livestock', wrote the philosopher Jacques Derrida, suggesting that without the transformation of animals into meat, there is no self-definition around which to cohere as a society of humans. And yet, it is precisely our knowledge that this arrangement is inherently social that dents our resolve to imagine human mastery as 'naturally' given. Contained within the thrill of the self-affirmation killing, there lingers the silent threat of having this affirmation punctured. It is there in the tacit taboo of eating animals framed as companions. It is there in the spectre of human flesh as tragedy's ultimate meal.

X

If the disembodied head of a pig is a recurring tragic prop, its significance is by no means static. Within the gorgeously disgusting Jacobean tragedy of a film that is Peter Greenaway's *The Cook, The Thief, His Wife and Her Lover*

Still from *The Cook, The Thief, His Wife and Her Lover*, directed by Peter Greenaway, 1989

(1989), multi-purpose pigs serve as staging posts in a ruthless, breathless struggle between love and the descent into meat. Made within a decade of *Pig Earth*, when Thatcherite politics were into their most brutal swing, the film makes a restaurant and its kitchen the scene of a bloodthirsty pursuit. Its chief antagonist, the spirit of entrepreneurial rapaciousness, threatens to turns person after person into meat as the meat they are supposed to dine on decomposes in their midst.

In the film's early moments, two lorries loaded with pigs' heads, carcasses, and fish surround a naked man who is shat on, pissed on, and kicked by gangster Albert Spica, the 'thief'. The man being kicked is the owner of Le Hollandais, a fancy French restaurant that Albert commandeers and returns to every night with his wife and mob. Albert is as lovely to Georgina, the film's eponymous wife, as he is to the men he humiliates. As he handles her breasts at the table with an utterly asexual batting motion, feeling her up with the force of a dairy farmer inseminating a cow, he asks one of his men if he might supply them all with some human milk. 'It's a joke!' he roars, without a moment's pause for reaction. 'It's a precious commodity … not a joking matter!'

Still from *The Cook, The Thief, His Wife and Her Lover*, directed by Peter Greenaway, 1989

Crushed, perhaps also bored, by her husband's extraordinarily oafish tendencies, Georgina begins an affair with a silent intellectual who dines at a nearby table. Between courses they slip to the toilets, the kitchen, the freezer to tear at each other's Jean-Paul Gaultier costumes. When Albert eventually learns of the affair from a disgruntled sex worker, she calls him a 'pig' to his face. He sticks a fork in hers and promptly embarks on a murderous rampage. The cook, a one-man chorus of sorts who guides us through the action, ushers the naked couple, this time fucking in a room full of meat, into the back of a lorry. The lorry, that is, in which the pork we saw at the beginning of the film has been steadily rotting away. As Albert bellows away from offscreen that he will kill his wife's lover and eat him, Georgina recoils at the stinking van as though herself being led to slaughter.

It isn't long before Albert catches wind of the lover's whereabouts – a tranquil book depository which, we learn, is his place of work. Albert's revenge on his rival, as he puts it, is to 'stuff him with the tools of his trade'. While one of his minions pushes books down the man's bloody throat with a wooden spindle, Albert rants about the dignity in his own predilection for food. He wonders aloud if this dignity will be recognised when people reflect on the murder.

Yet rather than living to enjoy this decisive claim on the woman he loves, Albert in true tragic form discovers himself a victim of karmic revenge. When Georgina invites him to the restaurant to celebrate an undisclosed special occasion, Albert is ritually greeted by a funereal cortège of everyone he has wronged. Marching in, grotesquely, to Michael Nyman's *Memorial* – an epic funereal theme first written for the victims of the Hillsborough disaster – they wheel before him the dish he so loudly insisted he would eat. Beneath a giant shroud is not the hog roast so constantly foreshadowed. It is instead the body of Georgina's lover Michael, dutifully cooked (surely Pollan himself could not approve). Lifting a fork at gunpoint to penetrate the horribly glistening skin, bronzed like a Christmas turkey and garnished with ridiculous salad, Albert is shown no mercy until he takes his first bite. Finally, declared a 'cannibal' by his trigger-happy wife, he is dealt his bullet in the head.

Cannibalism can be thought of as a form of social regulation. We are forbidden to imagine its enactment, yet its place in our imagination, far from being alien to 'normal' meat, may be precisely what gives that meat its aura of attraction. No gourmand such as Albert would be content with the tofu-eater's lot, and yet when his self-declared desire to eat his wife's dead lover is actually met, he is cowed by the ultimate revulsion. While framed in our society as perhaps the most basic of evils, so clearly a natural crime in its potential to disgust, cannibalism haunts every tragedy describable as a situation of meat – a struggle over who can be reduced to their flesh. In the Dutch Vanitas style of the film's lavish set – a genre of painting that tends to remind us we are mortal – commonly decomposing entities constantly jostle for space. It is only at the moment of cannibalism, of Albert's 'recognition' of what he will be made to do, that the seemingly natural order underpinning his power is finally made unnatural. That 'order' has allowed him to shit on a man, impale a woman, and force-feed a child his own bellybutton. Now they all stand before

Still from *The Cook, The Thief, His Wife and Her Lover*, directed by Peter Greenaway, 1989

him and invite him to finish the job. The thief's tyranny, we see, is not a mark of his place as most human among these animals. Nor does his 'love' for Georgina justify his implicit desire to consume her. Instead, we find him the product of a social order vulnerable to violent reversal, an emblem as sure as any of the hubris of making meat.

Perhaps I have myself been overly cruel to my victims in this chapter. Even Albert Spica doubtless does not see his own brutality as fuelled by sadistic intentions. Particularly if, as I have suggested, it is the system of reward and punishment organising economic life that provides him with the motive and means to pillage everything that moves. Particularly if, as Jacqueline Rose suggests in her thesis *On Violence and On Violence Against Women* (2021), violence in our time is a thing that thrives on a form of mental blindness. For Rose, it is the 'rift between act and understanding, between impulse and self-knowledge' that lies at the core of that violence 'epidemic' to contemporary life. Yet if so, we have cause to challenge those who position themselves as tragic heroes under the delusion that 'self-knowledge' is achieved at the moment we accept our own violence. It is clearly not enough just to look at an animal, to stare one's meat in the face, to show us our own brutality.

Rose suggests that our potential for violence is compelling 'in direct proportion to its ability to suspend anything vaguely resembling thought, to release the rush of blood that gives you no time for pause'. Perhaps then, there is a function for the tragic arts, albeit those of the harsher, uncensored kind, in recuperating space for reflection on that which the rhetoric of Meat Love denies. Perhaps tragedy can compel us to consider our personal implication in the current of social life, to weigh more honestly our powers of restraint against the facts of our material conditions. Tragedy is not there to 'suspend' – not expectation, nor feeling, nor thought. Rather, it is there to provoke.

That Albert Spica dies a cannibal can never resolve the tragic situation. Rather it merely literalises and makes visceral what was true all along: that within the capitalist system we are all – whatever our place in the species, class, or gender order – potential meat for those who at any given moment loom above us. Georgina, like a man who loves his pig, positively begs the restaurant owner to cook her lover's corpse, and yet we do not for a moment believe that it is love that compels her to do this. Rather, her entreaty – an act of vengeance more than care – sweats with the desperation of the loser's last resort. It is this cry from the heart that is tragic and which cuts to the core of whether a creature makes its way into our mouths. For the decision to consume another's flesh will always have as much to do with politics, as much to do with power, as it has to do with love.

HARMONY

Still, where Meat Love is concerned, there is always a modicum of guilt. A sense of debt on the part of the thief, a fear of karma in the iconoclast. Even for those resigned to the tragic supposition that with love comes inevitable cruelty, there lingers an anxiety to smooth out the soul.

The rise of the conscientious carnivore materialises this desire for a sense of the ethically even. What an animal gives to him in death, the conscious eater hopes to provide for the animal in life. This, you could suspect, is the dance of give-and-take they call love. Pensively, magnanimously, he martyrs himself to this love's relentless promotion.

The man now known as His Royal Highness King Charles III of the United Kingdom was, in 2017, simply a boy, standing in front of a geometric rose pattern, asking a conference full of agricultural representatives to love Nature. 'In the soul of the author', he mused, 'harmony's words like lover and lover through music and meaning are calling to one another.' He was quoting a poet-farmer named Dick Jones in a bid to communicate the principles underpinning Duchy Home Farm, the agricultural venture that in 1980 the then-prince transformed into a beacon of ethical farming. As Charles tells us in his extraordinary 2010 book *Harmony: A New Way of Looking at the World*, it was his own gift to introduce organic methods to what was then a monocultural aberration, jacked up on ammonium nitrate and ploughed into insensibility. Organic systems, Charles explains, effectively mimic the workings of Nature, an understanding he evolved through immersion in the visual elegance of ancient art and architecture.

The rose on the banner behind him at the Harmony conference, though drawn with an extraneous petal, recalled one of the central images in *Harmony* the book, namely, the five-petalled rose traced in the skies above the earth by Venus. This sacred geometry repeats itself in countless artistic wonders, connecting us, Charles explains, with 'Nature's harmonic balance'. The book is replete with sightings of the 'golden ratio' in many organic forms – the ratio underlying the harmonic beauty of Botticelli's *Primavera* and its oil on canvas counterpart *The Birth of Venus*. In the former, we witness the arrival of spring, 'the rebirth of natural wisdom'. In the latter that wisdom is sutured to the naked symbol of love. Charles gazes at the precious pearl of the goddess's goldenly proportioned body and sees in it the sure-fire intimacy of our connection with Nature's laws.

According to the now-King, poetry, art, and architecture can lend us a capacity for reverence. 'It is an experience induced by love', he writes, 'and love comes from relationship.' Without reverence and love, says Charles, we are 'un-anchored by any sense of duty to the thing that deserves our reverence'. What all this is leading up to is an image of farmer and livestock in happy, loving union. Fundamental to Duchy soil's fertility is not just the nitrogen-fixing properties of clover, but the farm's judicious use of animals. The animals graze the clover and grass, fertilising the soil with their droppings, while at the same time they 'convert sunshine into meat and milk'. For Charles, this is the opposite of an exploitative relationship, which, he advises us, cannot last because it gives Nature nothing back.

One of Charles's central influences in arriving at this ethos is, he informs us, Pythagoras – the sixth-century Greek philosopher he credits as being 'one of the founding fathers of Western Civilization'. For Charles, Pythagoras's teaching gives us a numerical basis for understanding 'the essential kinship of all living things', a schema for stating that 'we live in an integrated and harmonious universe'. What Charles elects to pass over here is that the primary practical implication of this insight for Pythagoras was vegetarianism. For Pythagoras, the Persian idea that kinship should imply a reluctance to eat one another was so commonsensical as to be worth spreading through all of Greece.

Another of Pythagoras's most notable legacies, as labour historian Jason Hribal has charted, has been to inspire an extension of working-class struggle into the sphere of animal liberation. Seventeenth-century Pythagorean movements challenged a nascent capitalism's exploitation of animal muscle; a nineteenth-century resurgence saw the establishment of formal animal rights organisations. In the Pythagorean trajectory, the idea of an integrated ecosystem of creaturely life culminated historically in a movement that connected industrialisation with the creation of an animal underclass. What this movement understood was that no food system could ever be 'sustainable' under capitalism, which depends for its continued growth on the devaluation of nature.

Organic farming may indeed be a prerequisite for the sustainable feeding of the world. Less obviously 'sustainable' or ethical in nature is the harvesting of animal life, animal milk, and animal eggs. Less convincing still is the notion that it is the sun, and not human activity, that 'converts' those creatures into meat; the sun, rather than forced insemination, that gives us a supply of their milk.

Yet for some, the royal leap from fascination with the visual elegance of Chartres Cathedral to the pillaging of bodily substance from nature's lesser beasts is a matter of intellectual achievement. Rob Percival is particularly sold on this manoeuvre, dedicating much of the first chapter of his book on animal killing to an appreciation of Charles's 'Carpet Garden'. Said garden, located at Highgrove House on one of the royal estates, represents, according to the King himself, a visualisation of the organic farmer's creed. Its fig, pomegranate, and olive trees, sculpted to resemble a Persian rug, exhibit the proportion and balance of ancient Islamic art, mirroring, as Percival puts it in appropriately Carolean tones, 'the architecture of the heavens, the geometry of the cosmos'. These gardens, he finds, betray an 'underlying intelligence, a set of principles which the Prince holds dear'. Organic farming, he concurs with his monarchical moral model, simply emulates nature's constellation of relationships. For Percival, these include, in all seriousness, a relationship of unity between 'prince and peasant'.

You'd be forgiven for struggling to swallow the idea that what connects peasant and prince is, as Percival puts it, a 'shared ecological ethic' rather than a relationship of total domination. Yet leaving aside the feudal and the monarchical mincing of words, we are left with an appealing vision. It is one that proponents of a 'natural' relationship with meat – the Pollans and Fearnley-Whittingstalls of this world – have considered at considerable length. Pollan, for one, invokes animal domestication as a matter of animal opportunism: it is a matter of evolutionary 'truth', he thinks, that animals choose to sacrifice themselves to humans in exchange for the advantage of protection. Fearnley-Whittingstall leans particularly deep into the logic and language of dependency. Of all the creatures whose lives we affect, he points out, none are more deeply dependent on us than the animals we raise for meat. 'We breed them and we feed them', goes his attempt at evoking symmetry, and they feed us in return. The relationship, he concludes, is 'undeniably symbiotic'.

This idea of a mutual contract is what makes the narrative of life at River Cottage so televisually sweet. When

View of the Islamic Carpet Garden, Highgrove Garden, 2007

Hugh curls up in his hammock amongst the pigs it is as though he is but a five-petalled rose, a flower to be pollinated by passing bees, in turn to propagate his benevolence. We imagine that to abandon those creatures who share his otherwise solitary idyll would consign them to a fate much worse than a place on the menu at his meaty feasts. The picture is one, if perhaps not of anything so grandiose as love, of affection and unmistakeable reciprocal advantage.

In recent years, the phenomenon of the public media farmer has exponentially flourished, encouraging us to appreciate the visual elegance of rural symbiosis. Julius Roberts, for example, is a millennial blow-in from London to rural Dorset with over 200,000 Instagram followers, explicitly inspired by the achievements of Fearnley-Whittingstall. Having decided in his mid-twenties to 'have a stab at my own River Cottage', this updated public-school smallholder slickens the image of Meat Love like few of his online rivals. Bursting forth from between his posts of exquisitely plated lamb meat are snaps of the grinning young fop with the living article nestled in his arms. Sucking pastel-coloured bottles as though they were his breasts, animals spill from what look like the most intimate family portraits to posts on how to melt their tender flesh. Sharing a biscuit with a goat like the Tramp with his Lady, Roberts instructs his fans in a harmonious way of life, defining in the visual language of the Sunday supplement stylist the meaning of you-scratch-my-back love. Despite describing himself as 'almost self-sufficient' (this despite his parents owning the farm, and despite his reliance on a retinue of goats, sheep, chickens, pigs, and dogs), Roberts's concern, like Fearnley-Whittingstall's, is to model duty to those who live in harmony with him. 'You're responsible for a lot of lives and their welfare', he explains to *Tatler*. 'It's a bit like being a parent to thirty animals.' He advises his followers to refrain, like him, from eating these dependents more than twice a week.

Similarly inspired by love to adopt the farmer's way of life, the social media star known as The Red Shepherdess (named not for her politics but her photogenic hair) is somewhat more willing than Roberts to publicise animal death. Where Roberts leaves unexplained what he reports his followers 'cannot fathom' – that he can be 'stroking that pig's belly then taking it to die' – the Shepherdess accumulates followers precisely by filming the complex emotions that harmony with livestock supposedly entails. Having also been bought a smallholding by obliging (perhaps loving) parents after seeing a lamb being born, this 'first-generation' farmer is committed to linking love of animal life with the custodianship of animal death.

'Every single day', she observes, 'thousands of people see how much love and care I give to every individual animal on my farm, so of course it raises the ultimate question of why.' Explaining the choice to dedicate herself to breeding animals for food, she calls upon Disney's vision of the Circle of Life. 'I strongly believe', she insists, 'that we live in a delicate balance … We are part of the animal kingdom whereby animals eat other animals. I passionately believe that meat is a central part of a healthy and a balanced diet. I know that by giving my animals the best possible life I can, ... I can produce nutritious, healthy, and top-quality food that I am incredibly proud of.' 'I firmly believe', she concludes, 'I can love my job, adore my animals, and love the meat they produce.' Roberts and Red imply not only that meat is compatible with love, but that it is a farmer's role in death that grounds their superior respect for animal life. It is as though the love that culminates in meat is a love more profound than any other.

It is part of such Instagrammers' claims to superlative capacities for compassion that they project a degree of distance from the taint of market conditions. But even for such farmers as these, who make up for potentially unprofitable farms through sponsorships, book deals, television series, and inherited wealth, meat is inextricable from money. If any attendees to the Harmony in Food and Farming conference were unconvinced by the business insights of an heir to the Crown Jewels, they would have been helped to choke down HRH's arguably blinkered advice with an education in the virtues of 'natural capital'. Charles's keynote speech was accompanied by an address from one his co-authors of *Harmony*, an environmentalist named Tony Juniper whose understanding of the human-animal contract embedded in livestock farming was perhaps a little more 'aware'. Rather than framing animals as mystical converters of sunshine into meat, as though it came from the heavens and not their own bodies, Juniper describes them as 'earners', supplying food between rotations of arable production by providing meat and dairy 'products'. Positing animals as at once both workers and commodities, Juniper draws on the logic of finance capital to justify the characterisation of animal husbandry as a practice of care for nature. By 'investing' in animals as sources of natural capital, he suggests, the human farmer and eater alike can expect to reap bounteous 'dividends'.

It would be possible at this stage to deny altogether the sincerity of upper-class 'love'. You do not need to have lost your home, job, autonomy, or dignity to financial crisis to grasp the distance of this economic system from any vision of a harmonious order. It is worth, however, staying with the relation between love and profit. For most farmers, after all, profit remains the necessary means of passage through life.

What kind of love, for example, do we talk about when we talk about 'mutual advantage'? Particularly when such advantage becomes the condition of our duty to others. Dependency, as artist and animal rights advocate Sunaura Taylor has pointed out, has been used to justify slavery, patriarchy, imperialism, colonisation, and disability oppression. Its language, as she puts it, constitutes a 'brilliant rhetorical tool', cloaking in its adjacency to relationships of care the exploitation of animals for human pleasure and profit, bringing with it immeasurable suffering and unnecessary death. Animals' living and working conditions may indeed be less degraded in the hands of Insta-farmers than on larger factory farms. The livelihoods of such farmers hinge less, after all, on sales of actual meat or dairy than on the proceeds of what amounts to an online zoo. Yet the standard of animal life in both – cheapened to the point of disposability – remains a product of the same system of profit and loss, just as it is to a lesser degree for humans who work in husbandry and slaughter. Love, as Taylor notes, is not an apolitical feeling, particularly where it is called upon to generate the impression that animals choose this fate.

Contra harmonious visions of animal subjugation as a 'cosmic' relation, the rhythms of animal life on any farm, however loving, are harmonised with cycles of production rather than any Circle of Life. The feeding and fertility of females is ordered to maximise (re)productivity, whether or not they spend their lives in the restriction of a farrowing crate. Like cows bred for dairy, sows are inseminated early and brutally often, and are typically sent for slaughter as soon as they are no longer 'good'. Fearnley-Whittingstall puts it as a matter of self-congratulation: 'We control almost every aspect of [livestock] lives: their feeding, their breeding, their health, their pain, or freedom from it, and finally the timing and manner of their death.' In capitalist time, the seasonal cycle of gestation, usually a rare enough trauma, is dragged into the endless time of production and circulation. Like the bottomless Instagram feed of the harmony propagandist, it insists that whatever we like to consume will remain at our fingertips forever.

It is in husbandry, Juniper's exemplum of care, that the implication of love in the violence of livestock farming becomes particularly stark. In an article for socialist feminist journal *Lux*, Sunaura Taylor and her sister Astra emphasise the patriarchal resonance of the sexual, reproductive, and economic exploitation involved in so genteel-sounding a practice. Marriage, they point out, emerged from the very first as a way of transferring land, livestock, and women as property to a husband. Just as this master could do with his possessions whatever he saw fit, the imagined relationship of farmers to their animal wives still comes, for 'consumers of all political persuasions', with the impression that it is natural and justifiable when built around love.

One such consumer is philosopher Kathy Rudy, who in her 2013 book *Loving Animals* insists with defenders of evolutionary 'symbiosis' that nonhuman animals are discernibly capable of love for humans. 'I believe', she writes, 'that emotional connections with real animals, connections based on love and shared lives, need to be included in the discourse of animal advocacy.' This approach is about 'animals loving us back. It recognizes that the animals have choice, and that one of the choices many of them make is to become loving'.

Rudy's analysis rides on an observation of what may indeed be animal pleasure. Yet as philosopher Amia Srinivasan points out in a discussion of bestiality, the conflation of pleasure with consent is a notable commonplace in rape apologism. This truth is worth bearing in mind when we consider precisely what husbandry involves. Unlike in human-animal encounters that retain the possibility of consent, 'breeding guns' are forcibly inserted into female animals' genitals, their cervixes flattened with the elbow or hand to put pressure on the vagina. Cows must first be restrained before they supposedly 'consent' to this process, a fact betrayed by the existence of what is known within the industry as a 'rape rack'. For Srinivasan, it says something about the hypocrisy of social attitudes to bestiality that the violation of animals for human sexual pleasure is outlawed where husbandry isn't.

From the perspective of animal liberation, meanwhile, it says something that the violation of animals for their flesh and secretions remains legal. That there is any comparison at all to be made with bestiality ought to be instructive when it comes to the analysis of power. For if ideas of male love and protection have been used to naturalise the domination of women, it is a similar system of domination that secures us the right to violate female animals. Love and affection may indeed be a ground for some farmers' relative mercy, yet love is itself insufficient to undo that allocation of rights.

Despite the aggressive marketing of milk as essential to the human diet, the vast majority of adults in the world are unable to properly digest it. Since most of us cease to produce the necessary enzyme after being weaned off our own mothers, there is arguably little that is 'natural' about our insistence as a species on attempting to maintain the digestive chemistry of infants. Particularly when all that is at stake is our access to the milk of animal species, meaning we must requisition it from their children (who we eat for good measure). While meat is certainly better tolerated among humans than milk, it is useful when thinking about meat to understand how it performs a similar function in the collective psyche. When Freud described the figure of 'His Majesty the Baby', he could not have foreseen the extent of its literalisation by our King, who marvels at sunshine's 'conversion' of animals' milk into a treat for adult humans. What

Freud meant by this archetype was that human narcissism – the belief that the entire world exists for our own manipulation and satisfaction – begins in our earliest infancy and ends with our inevitable destruction. As Jacqueline Rose interprets this insight in her discussion of violence against women, the 'baby' finds himself unable to properly love or even recognise the needs of others as he struggles with the mother 'against the dawning recognition that [he is] as helpless as [he is] dependent on others to survive'.

If we take seriously this idea, we are drawn from an imaginary of care towards an understanding of fear. If our own dependency on animal life forms the anxious undercurrent of our insistence that they depend on us, it makes sense that we would swallow it all down. We swallow to insist that we will not ourselves be swallowed – neither by helplessness nor guilt. Recognition of our dependency, our lack of self-sufficient freedom, provokes us into all manner of contortions to justify clawing at the freedom of others. 'Animals are just as intelligent as we are in their own way', remarks Roberts. 'It's amazing but terrifying at the same time.'

Such an anxiety might also go some way towards explaining the confusion of identity so often betrayed by those who work with meat. 'I'll never forget my first visit to the local, family-run abattoir', Roberts reports. 'It hit me like a train. But seeing how kindly and humanely it could be done, when done right, really affirmed things for me – they're skinned, gutted, and ready within five minutes.' Convenience for the human – the efficiency of 'preparation' and its overall comforting effect – is mistaken for the kindness and humanity of what is being done to the animal. In Percival's *The Meat Paradox*, an interview with one of then-Prince Charles's farmers yields the following condemnation of vegetarians: 'We need people to choose to eat the produce of a sustainable farming system, or else farmers won't be able to farm like this.' 'We need', the farmer protests, 'to get over the idea that all animals are bad.' With this linguistic stumble, it is as though the farmer has failed to comprehend that it is not the animals themselves that are blamed by vegetarians for their death. In a TikTok video responding to critics of her decision to kill for meat, The Red Shepherdess goes so far as to compare herself to a hospital worker. 'When you work with animals, or when you work with life in general … you know that with life comes death.' 'You have to take it all on the chin', she expounds, as though forgetting whose decisions are the source of whose anguish.

It is precisely in imagining away the existence of animal life, in rolling animal needs, interests, pleasures, and desires into the swamp of our own all-encompassing self-hood, that we establish a form of love whose culmination is consumption. Yet if we are honest about reading animals' cues as to their needs, interests, pleasures, and desires, we must be attentive to the means through which these needs are produced as well as expressed. As I suggested when discussing tragedy, the relationship between animals and humans has always been contextually – environmentally, socially, and historically – contingent. This remains true of the supposedly natural relationship of 'symbiosis', and also applies to the apparent animal need for human care.

Livestock dependency on humans for such needs as food, shelter, and midwifery is less a justification for animals' domesticated status than a product of their historical domestication. While animals, as Srinivasan points out, may signal pleasure in sex with humans, it remains a fact that they must often be trained into having it. Indeed, their taught enjoyment too often mutates into an eminently exploitable need. With that in mind, the fact that we repay ourselves for animals' 'need' for our love by helping ourselves to their flesh and reproductive secretions takes on a different resonance from that which the rhetoric of Meat Love strains so hard to create. It does not follow from animals' learnt dependency on humans that animals are objects. It no more follows from our crops' need for fertilising shit that the animals who shit must then be killed.

While this transmission of violence may be in part a psychological reflex, it is only through forms of social organisation that such reflexes are made systematic – standardised, institutionalised, everywhere set to repeat. The capitalist psyche may 'need' or depend on the exploitation of nature, but in large part this stems from the needs of the capitalist regime of accumulation within which that psyche is shaped. It is one of capitalism's central features that our primary 'needs' as individual humans are transposed into the need to accumulate money. It is only by doing this that we may indirectly obtain what our bodies actually need to survive. The system is therefore one in which the capitalist's need for profit will result in the unmet needs of those he exploits, extracts from, and burgles. The feudal lord burgles the peasant; the modern landlord extracts from the tenant farmer; the food capitalist exploits his workers. All human classes do the same to nonhuman animals, burgling nature itself.

Nature is capitalism's non-economic support – a resource that must be plundered, indeed destroyed, for value to continue to accumulate. This is as true on the level of nations as it is on that of individuals. Agricultural subsidies in countries like the US and the UK bolster the power of the industry to keep this plunder up when it would not otherwise be profitable. Subsidies depress the price of food internationally to the extent that poorer nations must import food they could otherwise produce themselves. The choice is no longer between farming arable crops and attempting to profit from livestock; rather, it is simply to produce and to buy whatever those more powerful have spared. Gentrification, capital flight, and corporate food regimes mean that those who might otherwise prefer not to eat animal flesh find themselves in urban 'food deserts' where meat, artificially cheap, is all they can afford to desire. The 'need' of the bourgeoisie both to eat and profit from flesh becomes the struggle of working and peasant classes to eat at all.

When farmers like Julius Roberts insist to *Telegraph* readers that 'we have so much power as the consumer to shop in the right way', considerations of manufactured need in the form of genuine hunger are fantasised away. Within a system skewed towards economies of scale, the products of small farms are necessarily priced for the likes of kings. Within a system that cyclically depresses wages, stoking the demand for cheap meat, it is hard to imagine a revolution towards small and loving farms not drifting back towards a similar arrangement to today's.

This is all, of course, to take seriously the claims made by people like Roberts that they want us to 'eat less meat'. One wonders why such figures have built their careers on explaining how to cook it. The agenda is not to persuade us how to console ourselves for our tragic carnivorous needs; rather, how to relish whatever superior cut of Welsh lamb the influencer has been paid to spotlight. The promise is that we, as humans, might master a better *relationship* with nature and animal life. In fact, what these actors promote is a mastery of nature and animals themselves. As philosopher Walter Benjamin wrote on precisely this subject, 'Who would trust a cane wielder who proclaimed the mastery of children by adults to be the sense of education?'

The fact remains that when demand for the products of industrial farmers is withdrawn by consumer choice, the system stagnates, jobs are lost, and the cycle of need continues. The entrepreneurial dictum of an ecological 'need' for luxury meat does nothing to herald an era of 'eating less meat' on a societal scale. Rather, it goes hand in hand with the unremitting promotion of meat *in general* as a kind of biological need. Large marketing boards are dedicated to keeping meat profitable in this vein. In the UK, for instance, the Agriculture and Horticulture Development Board (AHDB), the levy board promoting (predominately) animal agriculture, pours millions of anxious pounds each year into 'getting meat back on plates'. In a slippage of animal life and death typical of Meat Love, an annual campaign known as 'Love Lamb Week' encourages farmers, butchers, and retailers to 'celebrate lamb's qualities on the plate and on the field'.

These are just the kinds of slogans, merging our love of meat with our love of animals and of each other, that abound on the social media feeds of our big-hearted farmers. Their sponsored posts enjoining us to #LoveWelsh Lamb describe the lives of sheep fed with their mothers in nature, as captions to video demonstrations of the perfect Mother's Day roast. Just as we cleave the idea of our own responsible selves from our encounter with animal life, animal meat is spooned so lovingly and neatly from the bone as to seem to have come from the ether. The 'We Eat Balanced' campaign shows a squeaky young child and her grandfather nurture their love for each other through their love of the natural world. They are able, it seems, to cultivate balance with nature by eating a balanced diet. In one relentless, multi-version advert with a different ending for every species sold, the duo explores the wonders of meat by prancing with lambs outdoors after gazing side by side into the oven. There, a leg of whatever the algorithm has chosen is inevitably nestled, tucked in a cosy bed of herbs.

AHDB's consumer reports emphasise the 'rare' opportunity posed by Valentine's Day for meat retailers to push more steak on lovers and 'capture more of the nation's hearts'. Insight managers reporting on the 'romantic season' suggest retailer 'premiumisation' as a way of 'boosting processed pigmeat value', i.e., selling more sausages by marking up their price to something worthy of your special someone. The reports are illustrated with photos of supermarket bangers coaxed into heart-shaped packaging and cased in sheaths of bacon; ruby red steaks that bulge from their plastic, vacuum sealed beside heart-shaped pats of butter. The beads of human sentiment, labour, and desire that condense on the grain of this meat are mere drops in the waterfall of fabricated need through which our economy is sustained.

When artists Jan and Eva Švankmajer made their folk horror feature *Little Otik* in the year 2000, the young Czech Republic was well enough synchronised with the rhythms of global capitalism. Understood crudely, the film's retelling of a grisly fairy tale can be read as a parable of consumption. As it opens, a man, one half of a young and desperately childless couple, daydreams at the window of a doctor's waiting room. Babies, fished from a tank of water on the pavement below, are being thrust into the hands of queuing customers, hastily wrapped in paper like catches of the day.

That weekend, attempting to console his now officially infertile wife, the man unearths and varnishes a particularly charming looking tree stump complete with limb-like roots. He presents it to his overjoyed wife like the baby she'd do anything to have. It isn't long before this 'child', its defining feature a dummy-plugged hole in the face, comes to life, the hole transforming into a hyperactive mouth. The oral needs of this fabricated child will not be pacified by customary means. We see this first as, with the horrible, grinding grunt of an animal who has been starved, the child attempts to suck up his mother by the ends of her long blonde hair. Hacking her locks from the infant's teeth with a kitchen knife, the father begins to look concerned.

As the film progresses, baby Otik proves himself by far a needier eater than his parents will ever be able to feed, however needy they themselves might be for his love. From a pram-friendly log to a veritable Mr Blobby in size, the lumber of his body swells as he seems to inhale great bags full of bread and gobble down cauldrons of soup. The drama begins when his mother enters the nursery one day to find, beside her dozing little monster's bed, the shredded remains of the cat. A rainbow of pinks, a skeleton of lobstery gristle, its carcass becomes, for a moment, a pornographic object of delight. Suspended as though in thrilled horror at what the little tree has done, the camera

Still from *Otesánek* (*Little Otik*), directed by Jan Švankmajer, 2000

closes in to feast us on the image of its chewed-up meat. We wonder, as much as dread, where Otik will look next to satisfy his rumbling belly.

Unprepared to reckon with the problematic needs of her beloved tree, Otik's mother's reflex is to undermine the cat. 'It was only an animal!' she shrieks at her husband, who unlike her seems more than prepared to dispose of their 'only child'. Short of this, it seems their only option is to try and keep strangers away in order to prevent their bloody insides being flung against the baby's bedroom door as he swallows the best of their flesh. Eventually the flesh that is swallowed will, of course, be the parents' own.

The need for a child, excluding its role in the reproduction of the human species, is perhaps the most vivid counter to the notion of love as a matter of 'symbiosis' – the notion of love as mutual competitive advantage. For the needs of the parent are nothing the child can fulfil in the manner of livestock, compensating care with total surrender of itself as a resource. Rather, the dependency that characterises parent–baby love looks something more like the love described by psychoanalyst Jacques Lacan.

Director Jan Švankmajer during the filming of *Otesánek* (*Little Otik*), 2000

For Lacan, our need for the loved one is not simply driven by some evolutionary fit – some 'help' that the object can give us to further propagate our species – but rather by the need to have our own desire reflected back to us. Lacan's description of Love as the child of Poverty (*Penia*) and Resourcefulness (*Poros*) refers to the story from Plato of Aphrodite's birthday party. *Penia*, Love's poor mother, moves in on *Poros* when he is basically too drunk to stand, the result of this gesture being the Love that invigorates 'being'. All the woman has to give the man for Love to be born is the fact of her void to be filled. This void, reflecting his own, is a force of disorder that stirs his very vitality.

In *Little Otik*, the longed-for object is so tethered to this void that a baby, in all its specificity, becomes inter-changeable with a tree. Critics have read the film as a parable of greed – a portrait of consumer ugliness rendered in a spirit of moral approbation. Yet as Otik's mother sets about feeding her son unspeakable quantities of meat – bulging hideosities of viscera set to boil in gallons of water – the picture is far from any satisfying carnival of excess. Like Otik himself, the mother's desires are brutally unmet by the regular laws of consumption. As such, the film's animating force is not the justification of a tree-eat-human world, but the strain to resist it through a vision of love unshackled from the logic of advantage. We feel this, most of all, at the moment of fleeting tragic reversal, when Otik's father, having locked his son in a basement crate, goes down, chainsaw in hand, to finally dispatch him. As the man moves in to murder the child that has become his potential killer, he is stopped for a fatal moment by the tender recognition of life. 'Son', he gapes, for the first time truly looking at the creature, deranged by its return of his gaze. Too late, it is a moment of weakness in a society such as theirs, condemning the man to be gulped.

More than just the smashing together of meat, desire, and disgust, *Little Otik* is a film that harasses us to reimagine love. How might we begin to love another, attempt to satisfy their needs, without regard for where this places us in a brutal contest of might? The fate of Otik's father has already been sealed by the laws of his fictional world. Yet what other kinds of world remain possible in historical space and time? In what kind of world might our shared animality be taken as a ground for trans-species solidarity rather than trans-species killing: a concern on the part of 'feminists' for the reproductive rights of female animals; a concern on the part of workers for animal muscle and meat? The logic of 'harmony' that underpins so many representations of humans' love for animals is limited by a belligerent refusal to relinquish our entitlement to eat them. Indeed, it is a belligerent refusal to relinquish anything at all.

The Švankmajers' provocation, by means of both horror and humour, is to animate the extent to which this refusal endangers humankind – the extent to which fear and want, perceived as need, will always reproduce itself, driving us into an endless war against our own inevitable vulnerability. We see this not only in ecological collapse, but in the ever-intensifying misery of animals farmed for food. Their misery increases despite the availability of

Meat Love for those who can afford it. We feel the disaster in the deepening failure to satisfy our own desires, if not in the abject failure of society to distribute the excess of food. As for His Majesty Narcissus, drowned in the pool in which he contemplates his own reflection, so for all of life on the planetary scale.

Jan Švankmajer has lamented the ways in which surrealist artistic techniques were harnessed by commercial advertising, their once politically potent imaginative power absorbed into its brute, dumb logic. This perhaps explains his use in *Little Otik* of the short animation *Meat Love*, which he had made in 1989. In *Little Otik*, the one-minute film is condensed into a five-second television ad for 'Flora' flour. Two dusted-up steaks are shown together as though locked in a playful embrace, a quaint domesticity lent to the 'tip-top taste' of meat that has been dredged with Flora.

What we do not see in this cute, truncated clip, distorted for the purposes of nothing but a fictional sale, amounts to a miniature tragedy of love, anticipation, and loss. In the full-length version of *Meat Love* the two freshly born pieces of steak, sliced with a knife from a hefty rump, begin their embrace as a kitchen block flirtation. Gesturing with protruding flaps of flesh, they preen and shuffle and spank before waltzing 'cheek to cheek'. Throwing themselves with delight into a shallow bowl of flour, they play-fight, wrestle, and start to pound against each other's live meat until, in a single motion, they are skewered with a pair of forks. There, in a pan of hot oil, for the film's final second they sizzle and begin to shrink. After this, we assume, they will be transformed into a beautiful, motionless meal.

Lacan's description of love, given with reference to Plato's *Symposium*, contradicts the more basic understanding of the word that Plato attributes to the character Erixymachus. For Erixymachus, as for the now-King of England, the dynamics of love can be compared with the principles of harmony in music. Yet as Lacan perceives, to understand love in terms of harmony, compatibility,

Stills from *Meat Love*, directed by Jan Švankmajer, 1989

symbiosis, or other such terms of organisation is to ignore the power of disruption – the disorganising force – that love would seem to hold. When Otik's father looks up at his now-gargantuan son, the moment of derailment emerges, as so often it does, as if from nowhere.

In its narrower, Erixymachean sense, the idea of 'harmony' implies the system of rules in Western music that determine the acceptable, most pleasing arrangement of pitches sounding together. The more basic musical definition of the term, however, is in fact a less organised thing, referring simply to two or more simultaneous sounds. Here, the *how* of the harmony makes no relevant difference – whether simultaneity creates the sublime or an uneven, jarring scream. All that matters is that they co-exist, thrust together for interpretation, normally by whoever it happens to be who 'wields the cane'.

BEAUTY

If the beauty in the eye of a beholder tells us something about that beholder's 'milieu', what does it say about mine that for most of my adult life I seem to have been aware of a fashion for perceiving beauty in slurping marrow from the shin of a baby cow?

One is encouraged to scrape the marrow from its bubbling chimney of bone and spread it on sourdough toast. It is served with parsley salad at London's St John restaurant, and according to Anthony Bourdain in 2002, if you'd eaten bone marrow anywhere it was probably because they did it first.

That the trend for bone marrow in middle-class London has been visually led is surprising for a number of reasons. For one, it departs from prior, continental aesthetics in gourmet culture – the razor clean edges of filets and steaks perched precisely on dauphinoise foundations. For another, the men whose slurping we are shown as exemplars of 'taste' have a tendency for being unbearable. On his earliest televised trip to St John to spread the good word about offal, Bourdain was keen to establish his kinship with chef-proprietor Fergus Henderson. The men bond over a shared identity: being 'all about the innards'. These are often, they explain, the tastiest animal parts. In the adjacent Smithfield meat market, as they gaze upon the bunting of a cow's conjoined interior organs, Bourdain compares the snotty red mass to an Itchy and Scratchy animation – you know, where they yank Scratchy's guts out. 'It's all good man', the gastronome reflects with an air of great profundity. 'This', he remarks, 'is it.'

In 2016 we find Bourdain to be still on a similar hype, this time appearing over a plate of the fatty bone tissue alongside critic and studied bon viveur Jay Rayner. At this moment of review for the marrow, 'one of the most influential dishes of the last twenty years', the men remark on its remarkable aesthetic legacy in the world of food. They claim to have found in the calf's jellied innards 'a suspension of logic and reason' – one that would seem to facilitate a higher disposition to that which has the masses eating unimaginative cuts of beef.

A similar position is taken by self-described 'professional carnivore' Nick Solares, who on *Eater*'s video series *The Meat Show* takes a trip to St John, an establishment without which he doesn't believe his career would ever have existed. What's remarkable about marrow for Solares is that it feels so 'limitless in its boundaries'. He too is enamoured of Henderson, 'one of the seminal meat masters on earth'. As they point their bellies towards one another to raise a self-congratulatory glass, we are reminded of the beauty in understanding how to extract the most flavour from the humblest animal parts – to find, in the sphere of the limitless, an aesthetic of balance and constraint.

The philosophy behind St John and countless ventures in its wake is that of 'nose-to-tail' eating, a supposedly British tradition that by the 2010s had swept much of 'foodie' America. In a world where the 'use' of animals is assumed to be a right bestowed on all humans, what nose-to-tail means for Henderson, the man who supposedly coined it, is the 'thrifty rural British tradition' of using every part of the animal. Thrift, it seems, can be as much a sensibility as an economic practice. While suggesting it would be 'disingenuous to the animal' not to eat it all up, it seems doubtful that the prime motivation of the regular at St John should be thrift or a restrained relationship with meat: a single plate of ham will cost you £29, an entire pig £700. It is seemingly more the aesthetic stakes of the nose-to-tail ethos that constitute its raison-d'être. According to its own cookbook, St John's 'exhilarating dishes', built on the inner organs of beasts and fowl, strive towards that holy grail of cultural capital that combines 'high sophistication with peasant roughness'.

Yet while this aesthetic ought to be reasonably transparent in its purpose as marketing matter, it nevertheless has managed to maintain in twenty years a remarkably virtuous resonance. Before Rayner and Bourdain move in on a plate of pig's head and potato pie, a dish which we are told exemplifies everything Bourdain believes in, we are shown the head intact (itself another signature dish of St John's). On receiving the result, Rayner sees fit to treat the viewer to a disquisition on Britain's greatness. As this human sticks his fork into the animal, he remarks on the island's historic 'tolerance' for the Other. Lamenting his Brexit-fuelled suspicion of a decline in this regard, he nevertheless praises the country's superior 'democratic tradition'.

It is likely that wealthy diners whose diets and careers have been built around meat will struggle to truly connect with the idea of treating the Other as precious. This likelihood is reflected in the vagueness with which the virtues of nose-to-tail dining are so often described. In Bourdain's earlier televised visit to St John, a pig's head and tail are set jiggling before him, braised with onions and split along the jaw to resemble a gaping crocodile. The host states simply that this is 'what food used to be about'. 'This is a chef who *understands*', he says, never daring to articulate *what*. 'This is a guy who took a stand', he adds, without elaborating further. 'St John represents what I think meat cooking and eating should be', declares Solares. Of course, he needn't say why. The point is that, regardless of our means or whether the killing was necessary in the first place, we are able to rest assured that we have treated the meat before us in the manner of a beautiful thing – 'always to be savoured', as Fearnley-Whittingstall puts it in his ethical meat manifesto, 'never to be squandered', never to be simply lived on in the manner of the actual peasant.

It is not insignificant, however, that the animal from whom the It-dish of marrow on toast has been sucked is the calf. The nose-to-tail moniker derives its literal sense from the butchering specifically of pigs. Ethical meat boxes, sold like jewellery to the wealthy and politically bored, will frequently offer a trove of cuts from 'Native', 'slowly reared' pork: cheeks, steaks, sausages, bacon, legs, liver, mince, and skin. Among the list of curations, however, you will often find collections of veal, more specifically cuts of 'organic rose beef', to be distinguished from the veal of the 1990s. Back then, the excess of calves produced by dairy cows relentlessly impregnated for their milk (namely the males who can't be used for same purpose) would be kept in crates and fed on milk until they were killed for meat. Ever since this practice was banned, producers have had to let the cows roam 'free' and have their fill of grass. Yet for the majority of dairy farmers, who cannot afford to raise these calves for long enough to sell them, the tendency remains to have them shot and disposed of shortly after birth. For the relatively minor inconvenience of £9 per body, these early-days killings excuse the need to register the birth at all.

In 2018, an alliance of farming groups and NGOs in the UK came together to help prevent this 'premature' killing of what a *Guardian* investigation estimated as 95,000 calves per year. Their solution was to work on consumers by producing a desire to eat the calves instead. As Fearnley-Whittingstall is reported to have here chipped in, 'If you drink milk or eat cheese, it's crueller not to eat it.'

The human consumption of milk and cheese is considered a primordial fact that ought to govern life and death. Repeating precisely this marketised perspective on cause and effect, the meat alliance simply rebranded as 'rose beef' or 'rose veal' what had once been a substance of aversion. 'Premature' killing is defined, then, not in terms of a life led to its actual fullest, but rather a life not 'wasted' in terms of human pleasure and profit. What was solved was never meant to be the problem of killing itself, but simply the problem of killing without ample human extraction.

To take one example among many, Coombe Farm Organic, an online butcher based in Somerset, presents its products as something 'to enjoy with a clear conscience'. This is interesting, since dairy farmers themselves have shown struggles of conscience over the need for so much killing. The 2018 *Guardian* report quotes a dairy farmer without the resources to 'raise' her Jersey crosses for veal describing how she can't even feed them if she knows they're going to be dead in a few days. Such farmers typically enlist the help of a 'knackerman' who will shoot the calf, take it away, and burn it from their memory. This is of course the natural outcome of a system that subordinates animal life to humans' sense of entitlement to animal milk. Yet such truths are of no more concern in the privileged world of rose-tinted veal than the brutality of the profit motive is of concern to the one who reaps the profits. That the ethical consumer can *enjoy* consuming the calves that have been raised a little longer manages somehow to redeem, for him, the cruelty of all of those other deaths.

The persuasiveness of beauty and pleasure as indexes of virtue is a curious one indeed. One of its weirdest instantiations is a lingering on the beautiful 'life force' of what is plainly dead. When Carol J. Adams published *The Sexual Politics of Meat* in 1990, she was right to characterise the dominant culture of meat at the time in terms of a denial of life. Adams's 'absent referent', for example, referred to a form of casual linguistic erasure. To complain, as a woman, of being 'treated like a piece of meat' was to acknowledge the violence that 'meat' implies while disavowing the suffering of its actual referent (the animal). Similarly, Adams's 'mass term' described the linguistic refusal of the personhood or individuality of lives. When a chicken becomes simply 'chicken' – a term of infinity like 'water' or 'air' – the slaughter of millions of birds is neatly collapsed into the notion of a lifeless foodstuff. On the level of acts and images, life can be disguised in acts of cooking, seasoning, covering with sauces.

None of these charges of erasure can be levelled at the artists of nose-to-tail dining. Indeed, it is the visual reminder of animals' former life that most stimulates our marrow-slurping men. Part of their delight is in the very intactness of the heads that are brought to their table – the trace of that living love-object that has been conquered for their lunch. *The Complete Nose to Tail*, Henderson's cookbook-cum-exhibition of animal carcasses is replete with stagings of beloved meat as though the stuff were still alive. A chef rests their cheek on a gigantic tongue as though the tongue were choosing to lick them. A pig's head held on a plate is tenderly shaved as though by a caring barber. Two little quails, their heads still intact above their plucked and lifeless bodies, are arranged as though having a chat to raise a macabre laugh. A woman, napkin shrouding her head like a nurse, or perhaps a virgin, cradles a red-raw, child-sized body in her lap, gazing with maternal eyes at the space where it once had a head. If one were looking for clues as to whether the nose-to-tail phenomenon were sincerely as much to do with respect as with artistry and flavour, one need look no further than such images as these – or alternatively, listen to the punters.

Solares, for instance, is thrilled by what he takes to be the flavour of a beating heart. Groaning through a plate of oxhearts, hailed by Henderson as 'the essence of the beast', Solares meditates on the taste of an organ that you know has been in constant use. 'The heart has literally been used

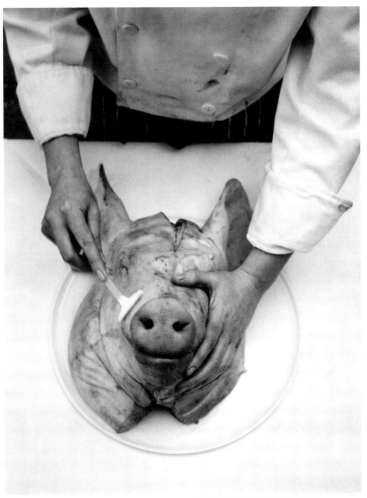

Jason Lowe, *Pig's Cheek*, from *The Complete Nose to Tail: A Kind of British Cooking* by Fergus Henderson, 2012

every moment that that animal was alive', he muses. 'That's why it's not very tender but it has all the flavour ... and all of the soul too.' To love the heart of another with all one's heart can indeed be a parasitic venture. Henderson suggests half a pig's head as the perfect romantic supper for two. 'Imagine gazing into the eyes of a loved one over a golden pig's cheek, ear and snout.' For those who do not have to imagine, the erotics of domination are plain. 'All the best foods stink', offers Rayner, craned over a plate of tripe and referring to the stink of death. The ones that most stink of death, he explains, 'are the ones that remind you that you're the most alive'.

In my introduction, I mentioned the twentieth-century unthinkability, suggested in Berger's 'Why Look at Animals?', of a spectacle of meat. By this I mean an incitement to absorb the image of meat not simply as an object, but as something that has been *made* into an object; not simply as something dead but as something that has been killed. Subsequent work such as Adams's was fundamental to exposing the processes concealed in static images of flesh – the tacit nature of the violence in images of animals

Jason Lowe, *Kid and Fennel*, from *The Complete Nose to Tail: A Kind of British Cooking* by Fergus Henderson, 2012

and of women. Indeed, if the spectacle of meat itself was once largely absent from mass media (low on animal torture porn or vegan agitprop), specular interrogations of the *meaning* of meat did then begin to emerge as a subject of scholarship and art.

Before the spectacle of meat became a subject of tongue-in-cheek marketing, its aesthetics were forged in a more critical vein. In the visual idiom of St John we find echoes, for instance, of Helen Chadwick's polaroid series *Meat Abstracts* from the 1980s and '90s. In these, precise geometries of offal – hearts, livers, tongues, and stomach linings – are arranged with a care and attention to luxurious detail mirroring that of a butcher. What distinguishes these pictures from a butcher's window display is a certain aesthetics of animacy. It is ⌐an animacy traditionally withheld from customers unwilling to contemplate death when purchasing their food.⌐ Nestled within folds of fabric and pressed against the cheeks of Chadwick's meat are various kinds of lightbulb, illuminating flesh with the aura of human 'mind'.

Helen Chadwick, *Meat Abstract No. 2: Tongues,* 1989

While we humans have historically distinguished ourselves by our cerebral detachment from the body, for Chadwick it is flesh itself that constitutes the site of human animation – all activity passing through the deep, red viscera sloshing inside the prison of ribcage, pelvis, skull. Like those we consider 'Other' for being reducible to the carnal, humans themselves, these images suggest, are comprehensible as 'conscious meat'. If beauty serves a purpose in these photographs' frills, folds, and illuminations, it is not to edify death. Rather, it is to reveal in meat its former status as flesh, site of our most powerful desires and, hence, beliefs.

The photographic installations that illustrate Henderson's nose-to-tail bible are an almost chilling inversion of this imagery. In Chadwick's *Birth of Barbie* (1993), gold nylon hair and lipstick-red breasts emerge from a vulva made of steak, plunging downwards as though towards an inferno of trivialised debasement. From here we reach the eminent piss-take of a soaring doll arranged atop two slices of beef tongue. The tongues, attributed by photographer Jason Lowe in an Instagram post to 'the profound and curious mind of Fergus Henderson' are fashioned so as to adorn this archetypically manipulable female with the wings of an offal-bearing angel.

Chadwick's *Meat Abstract No. 5: Heart of Liver* (1989) captures an animal's vital organs against a bodiless torso of fabric, strung together by the wire descending from a lightbulb close to the neck. Uncannily mirroring the structure of this picture of animate innards, St John presents (according to their caption) a 'young, keen, hardworking, ambitious' chef, holding a trail of organs by the lungs to his chest. Where Chadwick seeks to challenge the pretence to disembodied human supremacy, to offer a 'bestial reason to counter the ruptive forces of mind and money valued over body', it is precisely this 'ruptive' violence to which St John aspires. Its achievement is precisely to harness the body's aesthetics of bestial love in an act of mind-making-money.

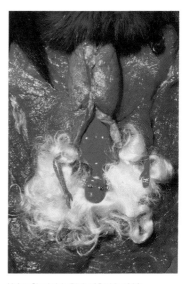

Helen Chadwick, *Birth of Barbie*, 1993

Henderson, of course, is not the only influential nose-to-tail chef. American nose-to-tail culture invokes not only the quaintness of British tradition but also the rural elegance of contemporary European poverty. Tuscan 'master butcher' and restaurateur Dario Cecchini arguably knows more than Henderson about love. Having always aspired to be a vet as a child, it was only when Cecchini's father unexpectedly died that he found himself in the business of killing (or more accurately, its products). Recounting his experience on an episode of the US television series *Chef's Table*, Cecchini recalls explaining to a mentor and friend of his father that, 'for me, to butcher an animal is a great pain'. One wonders how you might get from there to having a series of talking heads haemorrhage praise for your butcherly virtues.

The answer of course is an artisanal blend of economic necessity and the rise of a discursive fusion of meat, love, and bourgeois taste. Having been forced to find a way to make the family business work, Cecchini began to

Jason Lowe, *Tongue*, from *The Complete Nose to Tail: A Kind of British Cooking* by Fergus Henderson, 2012

cook in order to demonstrate to customers the potential deliciousness of cheaper cuts. The more he is able to minimise the number of cows he must buy, the more he is able to perceive a virtuous path for himself. 'The butcher', he concludes to the sound of soaring violins, 'is the one with the most important task … of teaching humans that you have to value everything', particularly life.

'He wants you to taste the *quintessence* of this beef', explains Samin Nosrat, fellow chef and Meat Lover extraordinaire: 'every drop of *terroir*, every drop [sic] of grass that cow is eating. You can absolutely taste the care that he has for the animals', she insists, and we can only take her word for it. Widely credited for restoring 'respect' to the butcher's trade. Cecchini's celebration by the gastronomic elite is matched by own his celebration of meaty beauty. '*Bellissimo*', he whispers as we see him use a knife to strip a pig of its fat. As he does so, he thinks of 'the life, of the respect

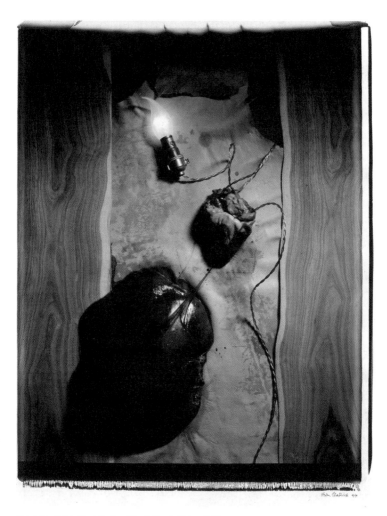

Helen Chadwick, *Meat Abstract No. 5: Heart of Liver*, 1989

… of not offending this death'. This, we are to understand, is butchery. '*Prosciutti bellissimi*', he purrs.

What this melding of meat with beauty, with respect, with virtue, with love displays is Meat Love ideology's remarkable capacity to elide various definitions of 'value'. First, there is the 'value' of life – often considered an intrinsic value, something to be treasured in itself. In cases of subsistence hunting and limited cases of farming, that value is perhaps less important than the use value of meat for human survival and reproduction. In capitalist agriculture more broadly, both use and intrinsic value pale behind considerations of exchange value. In all cases, however, the status of food in general as an existential necessity allows the mere invocation of use and intrinsic value to be converted into an exorbitant price. Even, that is, where the 'value of life' has been well and truly trashed. By mobilising all those aesthetic values we associate with the virtue of provision, need fulfilment, appreciation, gratitude, responsibility, and sacrifice, the meat machine is able to 'premiumise' its product. Ethical values, eminently convertible to exchange value in a market of guilty consumers, often misdirect our perception of what we should feel guilty about.

In Cecchini's case, the investment of beauty-appreciation with ethical weight serves as a beautiful means of increasing the exchange value of meat, albeit the meat of one particular butcher. While this may have helped him to compete with the industrial meat monster, the manoeuvre does little to elevate the 'value' of animal life in general. For again, as long as the food system is governed by profit, and thus continues to require that animals be killed en masse, the fantasy of respect for life involved in expensive offal is little better than a gilded leaflet for the carnivorous cause. 'Long live the meat', roars Cecchini as he raises a glass among his rowdy clientele. We sense they have not come to sample his beautiful dishes of flesh out of desire for a reprieve from the excesses of carnivorous consumption.

The perils of mistaking beauty for a materially ethical good are evident in many of Meat Love's illogics. The 'least bad' virtue of veal in the context of dairy-related killing rides, for example, on the fact that the cow has been 'given a chance at life' – allowed to live a while instead of being shot at birth. Yet the rhetoric of marrow-munching presupposes a system of value in which youth at the time of death is in fact the ideal. As one of St John's chefs explains to Solares on *The Meat Show*, the middle-cut section from the veal leg, cooked until the marrow is 'dancing', is all the more tender and delicate in flavour for being particularly young. The lambs' thymus glands or 'sweetbreads' he arrays before Solares on a tray are all the more beautiful, plump, and milky white for the infancy of the lambs from whom they were taken.

Our dual fetishisation and devaluation of animal life has become one of contemporary capitalism's central contradictions. In our aesthetics of the animal 'life force' as a beautiful, essential, fundamentally valuable source of life for humankind, there lurks an optic of humiliation that denies the value of animal labour, right

Jason Lowe, *Meat that Isn't Pig*, from *The Complete Nose to Tail: A Kind of British Cooking* by Fergus Henderson, 2012

to the land, or right to continue existing. We see this in what are known as the 'environmentalisms of the rich'; where the preservation of 'wilderness', conceived in terms of human entertainment, establishes hierarchies of species value policed by killing for food and for sport. Capitalism produces similar dynamics of hierarchisation in the expropriation of land from Indigenous peoples and peasants, and the exploitation of immigrant labour in the food industry at large. We see it in our treatment of 'nature' itself as a source of raw materials and curios for human amusement.

This contradiction is one of the sources of the industry's inherent tendency toward crisis. For to suppose that nature is indeed an infinite source of raw material is to make a terrible mistake. To suppose that animal life is a 'renewable' resource for human use and indulgence is to license the destruction of precisely those 'goods' that profitability requires for its feed. It is a dangerous delusion indeed to suppose it is 'life' that fills our bellies when we feed on the deadness of meat. It is in fact to mirror the dynamics of what Nancy Fraser refers to as 'cannibal capitalism' – a snake doomed to eat its own tail.

For all Fraser's invocation, in this phrase, of same-species taboo, it is not only human flesh that ought to strike us as a self-defeating meat on which to gorge. And yet there is perhaps no more effective counter-aesthetics to that of Meat Love than the grotesquery of cannibal horror. One of the least romantic examples is that of *The Texas Chainsaw Massacre*. No appeal to the human heart can save its protagonist Sally Hardesty from the clutches of a family of hungry men at the height of the 1970s oil and profit crisis. At the film's culmination, Sally finds herself seated at this family's dinner table, a plate of human meat in front of her and an assurance that she will be next. In an agonising sequence of hysterical pleading to make the atrocities stop, Sally tells her ghoulish captors she'll do anything they want. The men can only laugh at the presumptions of human sentiment behind this offer. They have no interest in her body (or her soul, for that matter) for anything other than food.

Set amid the hot, thick nightmare of a real-life economic trough, the film depicts the killing and butchering of a group of road-tripping teenagers as they wait to refill their van. Early on, when they still have gas in the tank and some sense of a viable future, one of them – Sally's

Still from *The Texas Chainsaw Massacre*, directed by Tobe Hooper, 1974

brother Franklin – points out the old slaughterhouse where grandpa used to sell his cows. Shortly thereafter they have picked up a hitchhiker, a friendly if extremely unnerving young man, his jittery cheekbone marbled with a deep red stain. He and Franklin immediately establish an abattoir connection. The man, his brother, and his grandfather all once worked there too. Franklin wants to know if he has been to the place where they shoot the cattle with an air gun, which causes the man to shudder and argue instead for the 'sledge'. The sledgehammer, he insists, attacking the palm of one hand with the fist of the other, was better. Whether or not the air gun's efficiency is 'kinder' to the cows, the fact remains it has put the young man's family out of a job.

And yet, if this family of men has been deprived of their dignity in labour, their skills in butchery, cooking, and traditional thrift are the stuff of a Food Network special. If according to Fergus Henderson the flesh from a pig's head is 'flavoursome and tender', its cheeks just sufficiently exercised and with just the right ratio of fat to ensure 'succulent cooking results', such insights are not lost on the family of Texas killers, who as the young man describes to his carful of teenage companions, never throw anything away. 'They take the head and they boil it', he explains, 'except for the tongue. And they scrape all the flesh away from the bones

… They use the jowls and the muscles, and the eyes and the ligaments and everything'. They boil it down into a big old jelly of fat and that, he informs them, is 'headcheese'.

Of course, it isn't long until the faintly unnerving man reveals himself as deeply disturbed. As he laughs and drags Franklin's pen knife along the length of his own hand, relations between him and the tentative teens take moments to go sour. Not that the youngsters would have been spared their horrible fate had they remained entirely friendly. For the out-of-work slaughterhouse workers are not just psychically deranged, they are also both resource-ful and ravenous.

At no moment in the killing spree that makes up this film, in which people are hoisted onto meat hooks and chased around with a chainsaw, are hints of animality in the parade of human flesh a source of reassurance. That human screams are seamlessly intercut with squealing pig sounds; that we cannot tell the source of the greasy red meat that turns on the family barbeque – all of this is merely to exteriorise in the world of some middle-class teens what was already the world of the average Texan slaughterhouse. It is a world of brutal 'realities' from which the family of workers has been slung, and now they must learn to survive on their own in the manner in which they have been trained.

It is commonplace in vegan activism to draw atten-tion to secret footage of the horrors of factory farms and slaughterhouses. It is to some extent a condition of build-ing support for animal liberation that the worst of animals' abuse at the hands of exploited workers is widely seen and understood. Yet the framing of these films as the cov-ert capture of real-life horror-movie 'monsters' disregards the systematic monstrousness that drives such unhappy work. 'You can make him stop', sobs Sally addressing the chainsaw-wielder's father, failing to perceive the abstract machinery behind the chainsaw itself. 'Just some things you gotta do', he moans. 'Don't mean you have to like it.'

Slaughterhouses, like factory farms, are often largely peopled by undocumented labourers, whose eminent exploitability adds injury to injury; the work of brutality is brutal, as the bosses seem to be aware. Annual staff turnover at sites of professional killing tends to churn at a rate of a hundred per cent. The cheap disposability of compromised and traumatised staff is a logic not incoherent with that of 'processing' animals for food. Research into the psychic cost of paid (often underpaid) animal killing has found consistent psychological trauma and widespread tendencies towards extra-curricular violence. If we accept that love is rare where life has been reduced to a vicious economy, perhaps we will be less quick to load the idea with such ethical weight. Perhaps we will be less prepared to romanticise 'thrift' among the well-heeled diners of Smithfield. Perhaps we will come to re-experience the stink of death as a source of something like disgust.

Texas Chainsaw's portrayal of nose-to-tail gastronomy – the verbal lesson in cooking a head that has Pam nearly throw up her breakfast – was broadly received by its original audience with similar revulsion. It says a great deal that within twenty years, the same lesson could have been

Still from *The Texas Chainsaw Massacre*, directed by Tobe Hooper, 1974

converted into a virtuosic 'redemption of British food'. Perhaps it is as much a matter for the analyst's couch as it is for Marxist translation that what then passed for an intelligible filmic sign of perversion could now have been transformed into middle-class taste; that what passed for macabre violence towards cows could now be understood in terms of love. It is interesting that fops, aesthetes, 'foodies', and even royals will go to extensive lengths to invent a 'poverty' in themselves in order to fill the space with love. It is an act that resonates loudly with Lacan's famous suggestion that to love is to give what you do not have to someone who doesn't want it.

'St John, I love you', whines Anthony Bourdain, 'and I need you now more than ever.' Over and over, needs are being whipped from the London air to be met through extravagantly humble rituals of poverty. For if indeed love, as the psychoanalyst would have it, is an invigorating affirmation of what we do not have, the way in which we express the 'poverty' within ourselves is crucial. For Lacan, if we want to bring love into being, including being loved in return, it simply doesn't do to look pathetic in our needs. Instead, our lack must be 'positivised' – presented as an asset. We see this in the groans of enjoyment that punctuate so much gastronomic content – groans that transform the primal grunt into a recognised expression of discernment.

X

None of this critique of 'combining high sophistication with peasant roughness' is to say that the hungry cannot feast, nor appreciate the beauty of food well-prepared. Yet there are many different ways of feasting, as Berger plots in his 1976 essay on 'The Eaters and the Eaten'. To the peasant as known to Berger, all food is understood to be the product of work, and provides an opportunity for rest. Mostly, then, the peasant will eat for purposes of pause and sedation. Nevertheless, feasts will be prepared to mark a special moment. When they are, they are composed of some special 'surplus' produced over and above daily needs. 'Expressing and using up some of this surplus', Berger writes, 'the feast is a double celebration – of the occasion which gives rise to it, and of the surplus itself.' This is because for the peasant all food, however special, is charged with the time and effort that went into procuring it. Whether or not one has reaped it oneself, it remains directly exchangeable with the value of somebody's labour.

Meanwhile, in Berger's account, the bourgeois eater who appreciates the 'value' of the life of a pig sufficiently to contemplate eating its ears as happily as its loin still remains unlikely to value in the manner of the peasant. For unlike an act of saving – an effort of actual thrift – the feast for the middle-class diner is always an *additional* expense. What distinguishes the food is, generally speaking, the amount of money spent. And as such, 'the true celebration of a surplus is beyond him, because he can never have a surplus of money'.

The futility of the bourgeois carnivore's attempt to appreciate the value of animal life recalls, at a new extreme, the futility Berger describes of looking at animals in the zoo. The disappointed zoogoer, always looking at an image out of focus, may at first suppose this disappointment to be a function of the animal's autonomy: 'It's not a dead object you have come to look at, it's alive … Why should this coincide with its being properly visible?' The truth, as Berger explains, is that it is the zoo's inherent *degradation* of the animal's 'aliveness' that prevents us from meeting its gaze. Where meat is concerned, our expectations are yet more outlandish and hubristic. It is in both cases ourselves we have to blame for our disappointment. With meat, we expect to find in what *is* in fact dead the image of something alive. We expect it now not only to bear in its appearance some trace of life, but, what's more, to radiate the love supposedly given to it by its killer.

Not only the killer; the eater too. For in experiencing all that 'beautiful' meat for which she has paid, the diner is expecting to catch a reflection of her own loving disposition. She is expecting to find in the colour, grain, and juice of her feast the deep satisfaction of a reciprocal exchange. Yet what if, as in Lacanian terms, love is not satisfaction but rather a kind of being? What if what is loved in another is not their physical attributes, per se, but rather something that extends beyond 'features'? Love, says Lacan in the first of his seminars, can easily turn into hate, an image-infatuation, not a gift but something inflicted.

Can we ever be satisfied into eating less meat by savouring beautiful images of its finest examples? Perhaps we ought to consider more fully the difference between looking and eating. For the philosopher and labour activist Simone Weil, our inability to look at something beautiful and eat it at the same time was 'the greatest sorrow of human life'. Only in heaven, thought Weil, might we eventually do both. 'Maybe', she wrote, 'vices, depravities and crimes are nearly always or even always in their evanenscence attempts to eat beauty, to eat what one can only look at.' Her point is that beauty is by definition that which withholds some satisfaction. Like love, it is that which produces a bottomless desire. Love lasts only for as long as there is something we haven't yet mastered – do not yet feel we have 'possessed'. Central to Berger's distinction between the peasant and bourgeois way of eating is that for the peasant, 'the point' is in the act of eating itself. It is inherently a matter of possession and thus can end in satisfaction. The bourgeois way of eating, centred as it is on 'fantasy, ritual and spectacle ... gives rise to an appetite which, in essence, is insatiable'.

The philosopher Becca Rothfeld, taking up Weil's disquisition on beauty, infers that the appropriate attitude, 'the only appropriate attitude' toward an object of beauty is hunger. In Weil herself, the inability to satiate this hunger produced a hunger for death. While to many it may have appeared that Weil, who starved herself into the grave, was the opposite of hungry, her impulse to starve strikes

Rothfeld as more like the longing for some total form of consumption – the kind of satisfaction available only with in heaven with God. Starving won't save anything, Rothfeld rightly points out, and comes to a conclusion that tends towards human liberation: 'whether you eat it or whether you cede it … every earthly comestible is subject to decline and decay … there is no possible remaining and no possible possession, so you might as well eat what you want while the dishes are still steaming.'

Yet might it not be possible to extend our sense of liberation beyond the confines of human? Rothfeld is writing in the context of societal proscriptions on female appetite – an ill to be resisted as a matter of a feminist struggle. In the context of meat, however, the fact that 'comestibles decay' has a different resonance entirely. That animals themselves eventually die is often given as a grounds for humans to control the manner of their death. Such lives are mostly taken in their prime, when the sweetbreads are all the more tender. If all that is at stake is a matter of human satisfaction, it makes philosophical sense to eat without care and to relish as much as we can. Meat Love, however, is never a matter of simple satisfaction – it is always a matter of beauty, and of that we will never be full.

AFTERWORD

Suppose the feeling provoked by beauty weren't hunger after all, but rather a kind of *desire* for which there is no nutritious solution. Perhaps, accepting this, we would accept the absurdity in making a virtue of meat, of gulping down every fibre until we are satisfied the animal it came from didn't die in vain. Perhaps, we might see, the alternative isn't 'mindless consumption' or waste, but rather a reappraisal of our most violently defended desires.

Desire and need aren't always easily distinguished. Within our sense of entitlement, if not for meat itself then for the freedom to continue to eat it, there may lurk a grain of legitimate grievance with a world no longer 'our own'. The middle class, for example, is not homogenous in its needs or experiences of systematic thwarting. Where once it was 'merely' slaves and peasants who were dispossessed while workers were 'merely' exploited, the neofeudal conditions of contemporary capitalist life are redistributing wealth and power to the richest like never before. Daily, the means of living are seized not only through the exploitation of workers but through monopolising platforms, rent, and hyper-expropriative fines and debt. Many of us live in a state of apocalyptic insecurity, precarity, drudgery, and fear.

Assaults on the welfare state in the name of 'deficit reduction', the plummeting of wages for workers and giveaways for the rich all contribute to a sense that all we once had is swiftly being taken away. Naturally, the impulse for many is to conjure some semblance of a 'feast', even if only to restore a sense of dignity to ourselves. Can those who can afford to shun the hyperexploitative meat machine really be blamed for the occasional indulgence in a grass-fed steak? An assertion of our right to enjoy what has been left on this earth for 'responsible' humans to enjoy?

It is often suggested in vegan discourse that we consider, in the first instance, whether our pleasure is worth its cost to animal life. On the one hand this makes sense from the perspective of class struggle, which aims to resist the unjust systems that offer comfort and safety to those who are prepared to collude with them. As Sarah Schulman describes in *The Gentrification of the Mind*, whether the benefits of a class society avail us as white or educated people or 'people who can afford to shop at Whole Foods', our comfort, safety, and pleasure often arrives precisely because others are deprived of what they need. It would seem to follow that resistance should take the form of a denial of such tainted pleasures. But does it follow that resistance should therefore imply a denial of pleasure itself?

For on the other hand, it seems there is little to be gained from framing our resistance to human-animal domination as a matter of self-denial. Vegan moralism concerning animal rights, framed as a relinquishing of human privilege, has done little to conjure visions of any society so transformed as to liberate animals as a whole. Perhaps this is because the kind of change this liberation would take would be more than a mass refusal of animal exploitation. Rather, it would take a social order so transformed that human and animal interests were no longer at odds with each other. Thinkers like Marco Maurizi, whose dismissals of veganism I queried at the start of this book, is right to argue for a politicisation of animal liberation – one involving a struggle for democratically conceived, non-competitive economies marked by solidaristic social relations. This should certainly be our horizon, rather than simply to 'veganise' the world. In such a transformed society, animal life would not be cheapened by the profit imperative because there would be no profit imperative. It would also involve engaging in the socialist struggle for a universal right to food – the enshrining of food security in wages, social provision, policy, and law. There could exist an alternative world in which no-one was compelled to feed on other species; where no-one could be comforted, consoled, or congratulated in asserting the right to do so.

Yet as the power of the Meat Love rhetoric has repeatedly shown among the bourgeoisie, our barriers to compassion go well beyond our actual material conditions. It is by no means a given that collectivising the human production of food should automatically compel us to extend this spirit to the species we have learnt to love devouring. It is not insignificant that human community, such as it exists, so often converges on rituals of animal consumption. If, then, it is true that animal liberation demands a communised social order, the question is how we can become a species equipped not just to carry out proposals such as Maurizi's but to extend them to ensure the recognition of animals as a class. How to become a species prepared to do the work of transforming not just human social relations, but human-animal social relations too? How to make that work as irresistible as even our hardiest comrades so often seem to find a slice of bacon?

As Butler and countless thinkers in the feminist tradition have suggested, politics must concern itself not only with the ethics of killing but with who is a killable subject. This book has attempted to show the extent to which the delusional ideology of Meat Love has *kept animals killable* despite contemporary concerns with meat as morally and ecologically relevant. Our ability to respond to the animal Other is discovered through bodily practice. It is crucial that we look at animals not simply to marvel at the value of their lives, but to value them more highly than they are valued on the gourmet market. Ways of seeing such as this are difficult to achieve if not through new ways of eating.

Sociologists, anthropologists, and philosophers have long been attuned to the ways in which food is a matter of cultural and self-constitution. As Michel Foucault noted of the Pythagoreans of Ancient Greece, 'harmony' with all living things was not simply assumed to be a direct outcome of a vegetarian diet. Rather, the daily practice of rejecting meat was thought to be a way of cultivating a harmonious disposition in the soul. The romantic pull of Meat Love (a matter of the flesh) attests to a need not just for abstract political *ideas* among those who would resist it, but for viscerally felt *ideals*, involving new pleasures and disgusts. In *The Use of Pleasure*, Foucault discusses ancient Greek dietetics as an active and generative art of entwining rational ideas with bodily habits. Foucault's particular focus is on how the Greeks exploited sexual pleasure as a means of designing social relations through the establishment of sexual norms. Pleasure in sex was central to the training of the soul to conform to specific ideals. Similarly, our pleasure in meat has whipped us to be certain kinds of social actors. As a result, a counter-ideology must appeal to our fleshly desires for something other than flesh. A just society for both humans and animals would require the right, in human society, not just to food, but to food that is composed of neither animals nor their secretions, yet to bring this about would require a culture in which we delighted in culinary pleasures that did not come at the cost of others' 'sacrifice'.

What we take this to mean among humans must of course be adaptable to circumstances, needs, and their accompanying conflicts of desire. As we have seen, the ability to mobilise towards a horizon of animal-free food for all does not imply a universal capacity to abandon meat straight away at all costs. There are in fact lessons to be drawn here from Pythagoras, whose aesthetics of existence were never a matter of universal rules, but rather of training body and soul to react to the shifting circumstances of life in the best and most appropriate way. Writings such as Berger's do not simply hand us new ways of seeing. Such perceptual transformations are acquired through practice. It is these that have the power not only to transform our objects of desire, but also to have us confront the question of whether the 'needs' for meat we invoke are actually our own. However we practice our politics of food, whether by making our own eating choices or by facilitating choices for everyone, the ways in which we eat are central to our readiness for social transformation. Contra the tenets of Meat Love, were we truly to extend our self-respect to the rest of life on earth, what kind of eaters, or lovers, might we become instead?

Capitalism alone cannot account, in the end, for the human desire for meat. What we have also seen, however, is that it is undeniably a powerful means of institutionalising that desire. Of institutionalising violence in our methods of survival; of systematising the progressive exploitation of the Other. It is part, but not all, of what entreats us to look at lives we think 'harmonious' with our own and choose to value them at less than our momentary satisfaction.

To free oneself, however momentarily, from capitalist and speciesist ways of seeing is to glimpse how we might live in the world to come. That our present society is a broadly loveless place – one in which acts of consumption are nothing but drops in an ocean of blood – is not then a legitimate objection to the urgency of challenging our taste for meat. On the contrary, it is precisely to reiterate the need for different ways of seeing, for different ways of arranging ourselves against all that this society has made us.

The loss that Berger described so sincerely – that of a respectful, if not loving, relationship with animal life – was, he thought, 'irredeemable for the culture of capitalism'. Our mindedness to redeem it would depend on a ravenous hunger – a desire for a different culture, a different society, altogether.

Works Referenced —

Books

Carol J. Adams, *The Sexual Politics of Meat: A Feminist-Vegetarian Critical Theory* (New York: Continuum, 1990).

Louis Althusser, *On the Reproduction of Capitalism: Ideology and Ideological State Apparatuses*, trans. G. M. Goshgarian (London and New York: Verso, 2014 [1971]).

Walter Benjamin, *Selected Writings 1: 1913–1926*, ed. Marcus Bullock (Cambridge, MA: Harvard University Press, 2004).

Aristotle, *Poetics*, trans. Malcolm Heath (London: Penguin, 2003 [*c.* 305 BCE]).

John Berger, *Pig Earth* (London: Writers and Readers Publishing Cooperative, 1979).

Judith Butler, *Frames of War: When is Life Grievable?* (New York: Verso, 2009).

Simon Critchley, *Tragedy: The Greeks and Us* (London: Profile, 2019).

Jacques Derrida, *The Animal That Therefore I Am*, trans. and ed. Marie-Louise Millot (New York: Fordham University Press, 2008).

Michel Foucault, *The Use of Pleasure: Volume 2 of the History of Sexuality*, trans. Robert Hurley (New York: Vintage, 1990 [1984]).

Nancy Fraser, *Cannibal Capitalism: How Our System is Devouring Democracy, Care, and the Planet and What We Can Do About It* (London: Verso, 2022).

Fergus Henderson, *The Complete Nose to Tail: A Kind of British Cooking* (London: Bloomsbury, 2012).

Fergus Henderson and Trevor Gulliver, *The Book of St. John: Over 100 New Recipes from London's Iconic Restaurant* (London: Ebury, 2019).

HRH Prince of Wales with Tony Juniper and Ian Skelly, *Harmony: A New Way of Looking at the World* (London: Harper Collins, 2010).

Jacques Lacan, *The Seminar of Jacques Lacan, Book 1: Freud's Papers on Technique*, ed. J. A. Miller (New York: Norton, 1988 [1954]).

– *The Seminar of Jacques Lacan, Book 8: Transference*, ed. Jacques-Alain Miller (Cambridge: Polity, 2015 [1960]).

Karl Marx, *Capital: A Critique of Political Economy, Vol. 1*, trans. Samuel Moore and Edward Aveling, (New York: The Humboldt Publishing Company, 1887 [1967]).

Marco Maurizi, *Beyond Nature*, (London: Haymarket, 2022).

Rob Percival, *The Meat Paradox: Eating, Empathy and the Future of Meat* (London: Little Brown, 2022).

Plato, *The Symposium*, trans. Christopher Gill (London: Penguin, 2003 [*c.* 385 BCE]).

Michael Pollan, *The Omnivore's Dilemma: A Natural History of Four Meals* (New York: Penguin, 2006).

Jacqueline Rose, *On Violence and On Violence Against Women* (London: Faber & Faber, 2021).

Kathy Rudy, *Loving Animals: Toward a New Animal Advocacy* (Michigan, MA: University of Minnesota Press, 2011).

Sarah Schulman, *The Gentrification of the Mind: Witness to a Lost Imagination* (Oakland, CA: University of California Press, 2013).

Sunaura Taylor, *Beasts of Burden: Animal and Disability Liberation* (New York: The New Press, 2017).

Simone Weil, *Waiting for God* (London: Routledge, 2021 [1950]).

Articles

John Berger, 'The Eaters and the Eaten' [1976], in *The White Bird* (London: Chatto & Windus, 1985).

– 'Why Look at Animals?' [1977], in *About Looking* (New York: Pantheon, 1980).

Sacha Forbes, Interview with Anaïs Gallagher and Julius Roberts, *Tatler*, 3 August 2022.

Jason Hribal, 'Animals are Part of the Working Class: A challenge to labor history', *Labor History* 44:4, 435–53.

Tom Levitt, 'Dairy's "Dirty Secret": It's Still Cheaper to Kill Male Calves Than to Rear Them', *Guardian*, 26 March 2018.

Becca Rothfeld, 'Having a Cake and Eating It, Too', *Agni* 90, 2019, 11–23.

Amia Srinivasan, 'What Does Fluffy Think?', *London Review of Books* 43:19, 7 October 2021.

Eleanor Staefel, 'Meet the Millennial Instagram-Famous Goat-Farmer Who Wants Us to Eat Less Meat', *Telegraph*, 20 February 2020.

✕ Astra and Sunaura Taylor, 'Our Animals, Ourselves: The Socialist Feminist Case for Animal Liberation', *Lux* 3, November 2021.

Films

Mike Dibb (dir.) *Pig Earth* (BBC, 1979).

Peter Greenaway (dir.) *The Cook, The Thief, His Wife and Her Lover* (Allarts and Elsevier-Vendex, 1989).

Tobe Hooper (dir.) *The Texas Chainsaw Massacre* (Vortex, 1974).

Jan and Eva Švankmajer (dirs), *Little Otik* (Zeitgeist Films, 2000).

Jan Švankmajer (dir.), *Meat Love* (Jan Švankmajer, 1989).

Plays

Aeschylus, *Agamemnon*, trans. Christopher Collard (Oxford: Oxford University Press, 2008 [458 BCE]).

Euripides, *The Bakkhai*, trans. Anne Carson (New York: New Directions, 2017 [*c.* 405 BCE]).

Television

Anthony Bourdain's A Cook's Tour, season 1, episode 2 (Food Network, 2002).

Anthony Bourdain: Parts Unknown, season 8, episode 4 (Zero Point Zero, 2016).

Chef's Table: Dario Cecchini, season 6, episode 2 (Boardwalk Pictures and Supper Club, 2019).

Cooked, season 1, episode 1 (Netflix, 2016).

Escape to River Cottage, season 1, episode 6 (Channel 4, 1999).

Acknowledgements —

This book was not spat out of a library, but chewed on, whether consciously or not, while living and eating with other people. I would like to thank my friends and family – the vegans I once trolled and the carnivores who now resent me – for feeding and being fed by me with such unrelenting humour, curiosity, and love. Particularly those who unflinchingly ate the Marmitey mushroom 'bolognese'.

I'm extremely grateful to Jess Gough for commissioning me to write something for MACK, for getting it immediately when I chose this topic, and for being such a sound editor and guide throughout the process. Louis Rogers's fantastic copyediting kept the whole thing in check, Liv Constable-Maxwell and Alliya Bouyis put it out there, and Michael Mack was a warm and welcome champion for the whole project.

Thanks also to the inimitable Sophie Lewis who not only offered a blurb, but also wrote thoughtfully and generously about the book before it was released in a true spirit of intellectual comradeship.

I'd also like to thank Will Rees, who informed me that everyone has their meat book, inspiring me to discover mine. And Angelique Tran Van Sang for supporting this distraction from working on a different project, and for helping me think through the afterlife of its ideas.

I'm particularly indebted to those people with whom I shared the arduous work of 'research'. Lucy and Matteo for always being up for a disgusting viewing, Matt for never tiring of River Cottage content, and my beloved father Jamil for initiating me into the cannibal movie genre.

I'll thank Matt again for good measure, who foreswore meat before it was cool and continued when it no longer was. He defeated me in the end. As, he claims, he does to all his enemies.

Pages 19, 22, 30
Stills from *Pig Earth*, directed by Mike Dibb (BBC, 1979). Script and narration by John Berger, photography by Jean Mohr.

Page 20
Sarah Walker (Agave) with the severed head of her murdered son Pentheus in *The Bacchae* at English National Opera, London Coliseum, London, 1992. © Donald Cooper / Alamy Stock Photo.

Page 27
Stills from *Escape to River Cottage*, series 1, episode 6, Channel 4, 1999. Directed by Billy Paulett, series producer Jane Stephenson.

Page 29
Spread from Michael Pollan, *The Omnivore's Dilemma: The Secrets Behind What You Eat* (*Young Readers Edition*), adapted by Richie Chevat (New York: Dial Books, 2015).

Page 31
Still from *Cooked*, season 1, episode 1 ('Fire'), Neflix, 2016. Directed by Alex Gibney.

Page 34
Spreads from Hugh Fearnley-Whittingstall, *The River Cottage Meat Book* (London: Hodder and Stoughton, 2004). Photography by Simon Wheeler.

Page 43
Still from *The Cook, The Thief, His Wife and Her Lover*, directed by Peter Greenaway (Universal, 1989). Still supplied courtesy of the BFI National Archive.

Pages 44, 46
Michael Gambon in *The Cook, The Thief, His Wife and Her Lover*, directed by Peter Greenaway, (Universal, 1989). Allstar Picture Library Ltd / Alamy Stock Photo.

Page 53
View of the Islamic Carpet Garden, Highgrove Garden, August, 2007. Inspired by small turkish carpets in Highgrove House. GAP Photos / Highgrove - A. Butler. Designed by HRH and Mike Miller from Clifton Nurseries.

Pages 65, 66
Otesánek (*Little Otik*), directed by Jan Švankmajer, designed by Švankmajer and Eva Švankmajerova (Athanor, 2000) © Athanor Ltd.

Page 69
Meat Love, directed by Jan Švankmajer (Athanor, 1989) © Athanor Ltd.

Page 77
Jason Lowe, *Pig's Cheek*, from *The Complete Nose to Tail: A Kind of British Cooking* by Fergus Henderson (London: Bloomsbury, 2012).

Page 78
Jason Lowe, *Kid and Fennel*, from *The Complete Nose to Tail: A Kind of British Cooking* by Fergus Henderson (London: Bloomsbury, 2012).

Page 79
Helen Chadwick, *Meat Abstract No. 2: Tongues*, 1989. Signed and numbered. Polaroid, silk mat. © The Helen Chadwick Estate. Courtesy Richard Saltoun Gallery.

Page 80
Helen Chadwick, *Birth of Barbie*, 1993. Cibachrome photograph. © The Helen Chadwick Estate. Courtesy Richard Saltoun Gallery.

Page 81
Jason Lowe, *Tongue*, from *The Complete Nose to Tail: A Kind of British Cooking* by Fergus Henderson (London: Bloomsbury, 2012).

Page 82
Helen Chadwick, *Meat Abstract No. 5: Heart of Liver*, 1989. Signed and numbered. Polaroid, silk mat. © The Helen Chadwick Estate. Courtesy Richard Saltoun Gallery.

Page 84
Jason Lowe, *Meat that Isn't Pig*, from *The Complete Nose to Tail: A Kind of British Cooking* by Fergus Henderson (London: Bloomsbury, 2012).

Pages 86, 88
Teri McMinn in *The Texas Chainsaw Massacre*, directed by Tobe Hooper, 1974. TCD / Prod.DB / Alamy Stock Photo.

Also from this series

Meat Love: An Ideology of the Flesh
Amber Husain

First edition published by MACK
© 2023 MACK for this edition
© 2022 Amber Husain for her text

Edited by Jess Gough and Louis Rogers
Proofreader: Poppy Coles
Layout design: Inez de Rijke
Cover design: Morgan Crowcroft-Brown

Printed by KOPA, Lithuania
ISBN 978-1-915743-03-9
mackbooks.co.uk